J.K. LASSER'S™

ONLINE TAXES

Look for these and other titles from J.K. Lasser™—Practical Guides for All Your Financial Needs

J.K. LASSER'S™

ONLINE TAXES

Barbara Weltman

John Wiley & Sons, Inc.

Published by John Wiley & Sons, Inc., New York
Published simultaneously in Canada.

Library of Congress Cataloging-in-Publication Data:

Weltman, Barbara, 1950–
    J.K. Lasser's online taxes / by Barbara Weltman.
      p.   cm.—(J.K. Lasser—practical guides for all your financial needs)
    Includes index.
    ISBN 0-471-39780-6 (pbk. : alk. paper)
    1. Electronic filing of tax returns—United States.   2. Tax returns—United States—Automation.   3. United States. Internal Revenue Service—Automation.   I. Title.   II. Series.
    KF6310.Z9 W45   2001
    343.7305'2044'0285—dc21   2001045524

*This book is dedicated
with loving thanks
to my family*

Contents

Introduction

In the mid-1990s the IRS started its *e-file* program—the IRS term for electronic filing—to enable taxpayers to file their returns in a new way. In 1997, Congress directed the IRS to increase electronic filing of individual income tax returns to 80% by 2007. It's expected that by that time more than 100 million returns will be filed in this manner each year.

Today nearly 40 million Americans already use *e-file* for their returns. That's more than one-third of all personal returns. Some use their home computers for *e-filing* but the majority of taxpayers work with tax professionals who submit returns electronically for them. These people have already discovered the ease, convenience, and other advantages of online filing.

With the advent of *e-filing* comes new ways to pay taxes and obtain refunds. Today you can charge your taxes as you would a new coat or a washing machine. You can authorize payment from your bank account. Complimentarily, you can direct that refunds be deposited directly into your bank account.

And the use of *e-filing* isn't limited to individuals. Business owners can use *e-filing* to meet their employment tax obligations as well as filing certain other tax returns. Various online options can help them simplify their tax filings, payment responsibilities, and more. Tax deposits can be made electronically with the use of a computer at an owner's direction. And audit protection can be gained by reviewing IRS audit guides online.

But online filing and tax payments aren't the only ways in which the computer has changed the way we operate. The Internet has opened up a vast array of resources on taxes and tax planning for the average individual. These resources can assist you in preparing your own return so that you'll pay the least taxes required while avoiding problems with the IRS. These resources can also help you take control of your money—by helping you not only with tax planning but also with financial, retirement, and estate planning. The number of web sites that provide tax information and assistance are well into the thousands. This book only highlights several dozen sites that have proved particularly useful—but don't feel limited by what has been presented here. By all means explore the Internet for new tax-related sites that are continually added. Of course, web sites can always change or cease operation so this book makes no warranty that sites discussed here will continue to provide the information currently available there.

This book is designed to help the novice move to online filing for individual income tax returns. This step-by-step guide shows you how to decide between using the telephone or a home computer to prepare and file a return. It tells you how to select software and use it to your best advantage—in preparing your returns effortlessly and filing online in a snap. It also explains how you can prepare your return yourself and then work with professionals to *e-file* if you don't have an Internet connection—even how to find professionals to both prepare and file your return for you.

CAUTION

Please note that the information contained in this book reflects the options available for filing 2000 returns. It is expected that many things will change for filing 2001 returns. You need to check web sites of the IRS, your state, and other sites for information relating to your 2001 return.

But this book can also help those who have already *e-filed* do it even better—using additional resources available online to learn the ins and outs of tax rules, stay abreast of tax changes, and simplify required bookkeeping tasks. It can also help small business owners meet some of their tax filing obligations online—to save their business both time and money. Finally, this book can help with long-range tax planning—not only for income taxes but also for investments, college savings, retirement, and estate planning.

How to Use This Book

Taxes are a complex subject, but using this book is not. This book covers four general areas of concern:

- Preparing and filing your federal income tax return—from the nuts and bolts of preparing returns with the help of software or online sites to the basics of filing them with the IRS electronically.

- Preparing and filing your state income tax return—which, much like the federal tax return, can be prepared and filed electronically with your state. You'll see the different filing options available to you on a state-by-state basis.

- Small business owner's guide to taxes online—coverage of electronic filing for business, employment, and other returns as well as using the Internet for help to save the business owner time and money. Both federal and state tax issues are addressed here.

- Using the Internet for tax planning—getting tax forms, publications, and other information online, researching tax questions— and getting answers—and planning resources available through the Internet.

The information contained in this book is designed to guide you on how to prepare and file your return online and how to use the Internet for other tax-related matters. It is not intended to be construed as legal, tax, or accounting advice. If you have specific questions or issues not addressed here that you can't resolve on your own, even using the resources noted in this book, it is advisable to seek professional tax assistance.

In the appendixes you'll find a directory of all the tax-related web sites mentioned throughout the book. These sites contain information, tax materials, or other tax help for you. You'll also find a listing of state revenue departments to help you with your state tax obligations.

Throughout the book you'll see three types of highlighted information to pay special attention to:

- **Caution:** A word of caution to help you avoid trouble.
- **Do It Better . . .** Some added guidance to make things easier and help you do things better.
- **Did You Know?** Some extra information you'll find interesting and helpful.

Acknowledgments

I'd like to thank the following people who helped me in the preparation of this book: Bob Shuman, who helped in the initial stages of this book; David Pugh, who worked with me to bring this book to completion; Donna LeValley, JD, for reviewing the book; and Elliott Eiss, JD and editorial director of the J.K. Lasser Institute, for being a sounding board on this book from start to finish.

Preparing and Filing Your Federal Income Tax Return

CHAPTER 1

The Basics of Online Filing

Just as e-mail has eclipsed snail mail as the communication method of choice by millions of Americans, filing taxes electronically is growing in popularity over the old-fashioned mailing of returns. The IRS's *e-file* system allows you to file your return without having to mail it in. There are several sound reasons for this trend toward online filing—convenience being just one of those reasons. The IRS has simplified online filing by eliminating the need to follow up with signature forms and W-2 forms—allowing for totally paperless returns. Also, advancements in privacy protection have served to enhance consumer confidence in using online filing.

If you're an *e-filer* or about to become one—for your personal tax return or for business returns—you should understand why this method of filing makes good sense. You stand to win in several ways—most importantly by making tax filing just a little less of a hassle.

In this chapter you will learn about:

- The advantages of online filing.
- The scope of online filing.
- Privacy concerns.

Advantages of Online Filing

You don't have to file your return electronically. There's no law mandating electronic filing. You can still file a paper return—through the U.S. Postal Service or by means of a private carrier such as FedEx. But using *e-file* to submit individual income tax returns electronically offers several unique advantages over traditional paper returns sent through the mail or by private carriers.

Ease of Filing

Those using their home computers can file returns with the IRS 24-hours a day, seven days a week. No more long lines at the post office on April 15th. Those who lack transportation don't have to leave home to file their returns.

Filing electronically is simple to do yourself—once you know how. Alternatively, if you don't have Internet access or still feel intimidated by doing it yourself or just don't want to do it yourself, you can use the services of a paid preparer who will submit your return for you—for a fee (generally between $25 and $50, depending on your location and the complexity of your return).

There are now combination tax return preparation and electronic filing sites on the Internet that allow you both to prepare and file at one location. The great thing about this arrangement is that there's no software to purchase or to download—you work directly through the Web. And the process may be entirely free in some circumstances. Even if you're required to pay, you only do so at the end of the process—when you file your return. For example, at TurboTax for the Web, your return can practically prepare itself. This site can automatically retrieve your W-2 information about your wages and 1099 information about certain investments if your employer and financial institutions participate in the TurboTax program. Other online preparation/filing sites boast that it can take under an hour to

Did You Know?

Nearly 40 million individuals filed their 2000 returns electronically. This accounts for more than one-third of all individual taxpayers—but still a long way from Congress' goal of 80% by 2007. But 81% of those asked said they were so satisfied with *e-filing* that they'd do it again next year.

Did You Know?

E-filing can be used whether you owe taxes or are due a refund. Two electronic payment options—automatic withdrawal from a bank account or credit card— enable payments to be made without the need for sending a personal check.

prepare and file your return—something that used to take hours doing the old-fashioned way.

And you can file your federal and state income tax returns in one step—*both* returns are usually *e-filed* with the IRS who, acting as an "electronic postman," then forwards the state return on to the appropriate state agency. In some states the transmitter routes the state return directly to the state agency instead of through the IRS. From the consumer's perspective, regardless of the technical way in which the state receives its return, the two returns—federal and state—are filed together, simplifying the filing process.

Accuracy

Filing electronically assures that the return you submit to the IRS contains all essential information necessary for processing. If something is missing or incorrect—for example, a dependent's Social Security number—the return is immediately rejected. This allows you to promptly correct the error and resubmit the return.

Software companies continually monitor their products for errors. You can download program updates to avoid any problems. Turbo-Tax stands behind its product 100% by agreeing to pay any penalty charged as a result of calculation errors in its program. Other software companies have similar guarantees.

Of course, assurance of accuracy on your return depends on the

Did You Know?

The number one reason that a return is audited is a mathematical error picked up by IRS computers. Even worse, math errors can result in overpaying income taxes. About 21% of all returns prepared manually contain errors, compared with less than 2% on those returns prepared by computer—and less than 1% of computer-generated returns filed electronically have any math errors.

information you provide. For example, if you fail to include dividend income you received, the math on your return will be accurate, but the information is not correct. Only you, and not a computer program, can make sure that the information reported on the return is complete and correct.

Quicker Refunds

If you've overpaid your income taxes—because there was too much withholding from your wages or overly generous estimated tax payments—you can receive a refund more rapidly by *e-filing*. It's estimated that refunds on paper returns take an average of six to eight weeks—even longer for returns filed around April 15th. But refunds on *e-filed* returns typically are made as quickly as two weeks from the date on which the return has been accepted by the IRS.

You can receive your refund even quicker—a couple of days instead of a couple of weeks—through a refund anticipation loan. This may be called a "Refund Advance" or some other term. But whatever it's called, it's really just a short-term loan that's being made to you. Intuit (TurboTax), H&R Block (TaxCut), and other companies work with banks to provide taxpayer refund anticipation loans up to $5,000 that put the funds into taxpayer bank accounts within two or three days of filing. There are no up-front costs for this loan—the loan origination fees are subtracted from the loan proceeds (your refund) that are deposited in your account.

While there are no up-front costs, there are fees for this quick refund method and these fees can be relatively sizable. Except in unusual circumstances, you should not use this method of receiving your refund because of the costs involved. By simply waiting a few weeks, you receive all of your money from the U.S. Treasury and you don't incur any loan origination fees in the process.

Did You Know?

There were about 80 million refunds on 2000 returns. The average refund to individuals for the 2000 tax year was $1,728. And nearly half of all individual filers received refunds.

Do It Better . . .

Instead of receiving a refund check by mail and then having to deposit it in your bank account, you can shortcut the process by requesting that your refund be directly deposited in your account. Simply provide the necessary routing information on your return (your account number and other information) and the refund will be automatically deposited in your account.

Acknowledgment

Proof of filing is important for several reasons. It assures you that any refund due you is in progress—you can anticipate its receipt to pay your bills, plan a vacation, or make an investment.

Proof that a return has been filed is also important in establishing a statute of limitations—the time in which the IRS can audit your return. If the IRS says that no return has been filed and you lack proof to the contrary, then the IRS has an unlimited time to question your return and claim you owe back taxes—whether or not you agree.

When filing a paper return, you can have proof that your return was filed by obtaining a registered or certified receipt from the U.S. Postal Service showing when the return was mailed. Proof of filing can also be a receipt from an authorized private delivery carrier providing the following services:

- Airborne Express (Overnight Air Express Service, Next Afternoon Service, and Second Day Service).
- DHL Worldwide Express (DHL "Same Day" Service and DHL USA Overnight).
- Federal Express (FedEx Priority Overnight, FedEx Standard Overnight, and FedEx 2Day).
- United Parcel Service (UPS Next Day Air, UPS Next Day Air Saver, UPS 2nd Day Air, and UPS 2nd Day A.M.)

Did You Know?

The IRS has three years after your return is filed to assess additional taxes. When you file a return before the due date, however, the three-year period starts from the due date, generally April 15th for individuals.

CAUTION

Don't wait until April 15th to *e-file*. A return filed electronically is timely filed if it has the electronic date and time stamp as of April 15th. But since it can take up to 48 hours to receive an acknowledgment from the IRS, it is suggested that the return be submitted no later than April 13th in order to make sure it's not rejected and you miss the deadline.

Filing a paper return in this manner—through the post office or an authorized private carrier—means that the return is treated as filed when it is mailed (rather than on the date it is delivered). The cost for receipts from the post office or service from a private carrier can be a couple of dollars or more—depending on the size of your return and the delivery method you select.

But with *e-filing*, the IRS provides proof within 48 hours of submission that the return has been received—at no additional cost to you. You receive an acknowledgment in the form of an electronic date and time stamp receipt for the acceptance of your return. Once issued, the IRS cannot come back later on to claim it never received your return.

You can find out about *e-filing* your federal income tax return as well as *e-filing* other federal returns at the IRS web site (www.irs.gov). Throughout this book you will see a reference to this web site—it's one of the more popular sites online, receiving more than 1.5 billion hits between January 1 and April 16, 2001.

Scope of Online Filing

Your individual income tax return can be filed electronically. Whether you file a short form—Form 1040EZ or Form 1040A—or the long form—Form 1040—you can use *e-filing*. (The filing of state income tax returns is discussed in Part 2 and the filing of business returns is discussed in Part 3.) Almost all additional forms and schedules that accompany the basic federal individual tax form can be filed electronically.

Paperless Returns

You can file a return electronically without having to affix your signature to the return or submit a follow-up signature form. You don't have to send in W-2 forms or other information returns showing federal income tax withholding. Your only electronic submission is your return.

SELF-SELECT PIN FOR *E-FILE*.   The IRS lets you choose a personal identification number that, along with other information, replaces your signature. In effect, your self-select PIN for *e-file* becomes your tax signature. Some taxpayers, however, cannot use the self-select PIN and must follow up their electronic filing with certain submissions. The self-select PIN is explained in greater detail in Chapter 3.

Online Payment Options

If you owe taxes, you don't have to send in a check for payment (although you still can if you want to). You now have other online payment options you can use to pay your taxes. And the IRS doesn't charge you anything extra for using these alternative payment methods.

- Credit card payment—you can authorize payment by Discover, MasterCard, or American Express (VISA does not participate in this tax payment program). TurboTax and TurboTax for Mac users can automatically pay by Discover Card when they *e-file* with this software. For all others, credit card payment is made through a telephone authorization or online through authorized credit card payment companies that charge a fee.

- Bank account debit—you can authorize that the tax be debited from your bank account by supplying the necessary bank information.

Payment methods and how to use them are discussed in greater detail in Chapters 2 and 3.

You Can't Use Online Filing If . . .

There are now only a few situations in which you can't use *e-filing* for your personal income tax return.

Did You Know?

In 2001, 231,000 income tax payments on 2000 returns were charged to a credit card—24% more than in 2000. The average tax payment charged was $3,085—for a total amount of $712 million. The largest single charge was about $2.9 million!

- You file your return after October 15, 2002 (the final extension deadline for 2001 returns). At present, this is the IRS cutoff for *e-filing*. However, this deadline may be extended in the future.

- You need to file certain forms and schedules that aren't accepted electronically. To date, these include forms that require signatures by parties other than the taxpayer—for example, Form 2120, *Multiple Support Declaration*, used to allocate the dependency exemption for a person who is supported by more than one individual (the supporter(s) who is *not* claiming the exemption must sign the declaration), Form 8283, *Noncash Charitable Contributions*, used for appraisals of property donations to charity in excess of a certain value, (the taxpayer needs the signature of an appraiser and the signature of the charitable organization in certain cases), and Form 8332, *Release of Claim to Exemption for Child of Divorced or Separated Parents*, used when the custodial parent waives the right to claim the exemption for the child (the noncustodial parent/taxpayer needs the signature of the custodial parent).

CAUTION

As the IRS works to encourage *e-filing*, it adds new forms and schedules each year. Currently more than 100 forms and schedules are accepted through *e-filing*. Be sure to check on whether any of the "can't file" forms can now be processed online.

Telephone Filing

As part of the *e-file* system, some taxpayers can use the telephone as the filing method for their return. The beauty of this filing method is that no computer or Internet access is required. There are no filing fees or costs.

Taxpayers who are eligible to file the simplest income tax return— Form 1040EZ—can use a Touch-Tone phone to access a toll-free number where they key in their wages, interest income, and taxes withheld to complete their return anytime of the day—or night. The IRS then figures the tax and remits a refund check or sends a bill for taxes due. This filing method is explained in Chapter 3.

Privacy Concerns

Whenever you use the Internet—to send e-mail, order goods, or enter chat rooms—there's always a concern that your privacy can be invaded. Someone out there with the ability to hack can obtain your most personal information and use it to your detriment. Perhaps the most serious concern is that someone will obtain your Social Security number and other key information to steal your identity—using your information to get credit that you're unaware of and run up debt that you can be liable for unless you can show identity theft.

In the past these concerns were very real—in the 1999 tax return season, for example, one online commercial site mixed up some taxpayer returns so that those who started to prepare returns online were given other taxpayers' information when they returned to complete their returns. And it was reported that the IRS site itself was vulnerable to hackers even though this is a violation of federal law under the Computer Fraud and Abuse Act of 1986 that authorizes criminal prosecution for violators.

Fortunately, security—said to be one of the main reasons why more people don't *e-file*—has been beefed up. During the 2000 tax return season there were no reports that any security was breached—either at commercial sites or the IRS. At every web site you log onto for preparing returns online and/or for *e-filing*, you'll see the security symbol displayed—a key in the lower right hand screen of your computer. This symbol means that the site uses industry-standard Secure Socket Layer—SSL-encryption technology to protect your personal information.

If you have any questions about your privacy at the IRS web site, you can send them to the Office of the Privacy Advocate of the IRS at CL:PA Room 7050, 1111 Constitution Avenue, NW, Washington, DC 20224.

CAUTION

Some sites do not use your financial data for any of its marketing. For example, the IRS web site specifically states that it will not collect personal information about anyone visiting its site. The IRS also does not use "cookies" (a file placed on your hard drive to allow a web site to monitor your use of the site). Other sites—especially those offering free services—request your permission to use the data for commercial purposes (or use the date unless you say otherwise).

CHAPTER 2

Preparing Your Return

The annual ritual of tax return preparation is dreaded by almost everyone. The job is tedious and can be extremely time consuming. Taking into account the time it takes to learn about new developments, fill in the form, figure the tax, and photocopy and assemble the return, the IRS estimates that it takes more than 13 hours to ready the Form 1040 for filing! And the more forms and schedules that have to be attached, the longer the process becomes.

But preparing your return can be a less painful experience, and perhaps even a pleasant one, through the help of technology—or professional assistance. With the click of a mouse you can use your home computer to complete your return and get it ready for filing. More than 6.6 million individuals used their home computers to file their 2000 returns. You can prepare and file your return in one easy step—with your computer or, in some cases, your telephone.

In this chapter you'll learn about:

- Return preparation options.
- Selecting tax software.
- Using tax software.

- Preparing returns online.
- Returns by telephone.
- Avoiding common mistakes in online return preparation.

Return Preparation Options

In the not-so-distant past, if you prepared your own return you had to gather the forms and schedules you'd need. Then you would sit down with plenty of scrap paper and, perhaps, a handheld calculator to fill in the lines and add up the numbers. After you'd worked through the form, if you found an omission or mistake you'd have to recalculate all your figures to finish up. The whole experience was time-consuming, tiring, and frustrating. Your only option in the past was to turn to a tax professional—in many cases a costly alternative.

Today, the process has been greatly simplified through the use of tax preparation software, web-based options, and other methods. There are a number of ways to prepare your return—some of which are online while others are not:

- By hand—the old fashioned way by filling in the information with pen or pencil. Alternatively, you can fill in forms at the IRS web site that can then be printed and filed—you can't save filled-in forms to your hard drive. The by-hand method is rapidly disappearing as taxpayers wise-up to their other options.

- Using a professional paid preparer—an accountant, enrolled agent, or storefront operation (such as H&R Block). This method is used by those who have highly complex returns, those who don't want to be bothered with return preparation, those who want expert personal assistance, or those who simply haven't stepped up to other alternatives.

Did You Know?

In 2001, about 57% of all individuals used paid preparers to complete and file their 2000 income tax returns. Some of the reasons people give are that taxes are too complex, they don't have the time, and they're afraid of overlooking tax-saving opportunities. But you can easily address these reasons if you use your computer to prepare and file your return.

> **Do It Better . . .**
>
> You may be eligible for *free* tax return preparation and filing. For example, seniors who are middle- or low-income can receive free assistance with federal and state income tax returns at over 10,000 locations nationwide (click on www.aarp.org/taxaide or call 888-227-7669). Some employers may offer tax preparation and *e-filing* as an employee benefit.

- With tax return preparation software for your home computer—a PC or Mac format—you can use commercial software to complete a return, one that can be filed by mail or online.
- Online—at commercial sites that let you complete and file your return in one place.
- Over the telephone—if you're eligible to use the simplest form, you can key in your tax information and let the IRS do the rest—figure your tax and send you a refund or a bill for additional payment.

Selecting Tax Software

Whether or not you plan to file your return online, using commercial software to prepare your return can be a wise move. It enables you to:

- Complete all necessary information—so the return is ready for filing. This will ensure that the return won't be rejected if filed electronically or questioned for missing data if mailed.
- Compute tax liability—including adjustments each time you add or change information on the form during the preparation process. The software gives you a running total—showing your refund amount or tax due as you go through the return. This information is displayed prominently in a particular location—generally the upper right or lower right corner on your screen.
- Learn about what's new in the tax law and on the return. Things change every year—with or without legislation. Software automatically cues you in on these changes so nothing is overlooked.

- Catch mistakes—a check or final review of the return will point out omissions that can indicate an incomplete return. The software generally prevents you from making a mistake—you have to override what the software calculates if you want to make any deviations from the norm.

- Red flag audit triggers. The software zeros in on areas most sensitive to IRS questions, such as the home office deduction. This allows you to make sure you're entitled to the position you've taken on the return so even if you should be questioned, you'll be secure in the fact that you are in the right.

If you plan to file your return online, you *must* use computer software to prepare your return (unless you're eligible for *TeleFile* explained later in this chapter). You cannot *e-file* a hand-prepared return.

SOFTWARE OPTIONS.   There is no official IRS software for tax return preparation. You must buy or use commercial software for this purpose. However, software sold for tax preparation must meet IRS criteria so that tax forms completed by the software conform to IRS specifications. Software conforming to IRS standards displays the *e-file* symbol (see Figure 2.1).

There are a number of software products available—some new ones may appear in addition to those listed. How do you choose from among the large number of products available? Factors to consider when selecting your software include the following:

- **Ease of use.** How easy is it to learn the program? Most tax preparation software today is intuitive—you simply follow logical progressions and prompts from the software to proceed through the program. How easy is it to navigate your way through the program? For example, can you jump to and from different forms?

Did You Know?

It's been estimated that about 10% of individuals *overpay* their taxes because they make math errors when preparing their returns. Since software dramatically cuts the percentage of errors to less than 2%, using software means you won't pay more than you have to.

FIGURE 2.1 *E-file* logo.

- **Cost.** The cost of software varies with the product you select. The more sophisticated the program—for example, a program enabling you to prepare business returns—the more you'll pay. But the cost of software is rather modest—typically under $50—considerably less than you'd pay for professional assistance. And, each year software vendors run promotions that can reduce your cost even further.

- **Integration.** Can you import data from a prior return? From financial programs such as Quicken or MS Money? How much integration is there with the Web—to import W-2 and 1099 information, to gain additional information, to tap resources, or file online?

- **Breadth of coverage.** Does the software do everything you need it to do? For example, if you're a sole proprietor, can the software prepare your Schedule C, including depreciation schedules and qualified retirement plan contributions? Does the software let you prepare W-2 and/or 1099 information returns for your employees, independent contractors, and others you pay?

- **Help.** How much help is available through the help button? With additional resources

> **CAUTION**
>
> You must buy new tax return preparation software each year. Last year's software can't be used for this year's return, even if there are only minor changes in the tax form or tax law—it just won't work.

Do It Better . . .

Don't forget to deduct the cost of software as a miscellaneous itemized expense if you itemize deductions. *When* you claim the deduction depends on when you purchase the software. If you buy the software for preparing your 2001 return in December 2001, you can deduct it on your 2001 return. If you make the purchase in January 2002, it won't be deductible until you prepare your 2002 return.

within the program? Through outside tax professionals? Through tech support? Some software now offers the option of live, professional help—for an added fee.

SOFTWARE PRODUCTS. Table 2.1 lists the types of software products you can use to prepare your tax return.

Feeling overwhelmed by your software options and don't know how to make an informed decision? You can look at product reviews that generally appear around the first of the year at:

- Eopinions.com (www.eopinions.com/finc-Taxes).
- PC Magazine (www.zdnet.com/pcmag).

Using Tax Software

There are two basic approaches that software lets you follow in completing your return:

- *Interview approach*—the software poses questions that you answer to complete the return. At each prompt you respond—generally with a yes or no answer or a number.

- *Forms approach*—you complete each form and schedule you select from a menu of forms and schedules. Use this approach if you are familiar with completing your return, know about new law changes, and are completely confident that you won't overlook any filing opportunities.

Example

The software asks "What is your filing status?" and you click on the appropriate box that answers the question. If you're unsure of the answer you click on the "help" or "guide me" icons to receive additional prompts. For instance, if you don't know your filing status, the "guide me" format on TurboTax asks a series of questions, including marital status on December 31st and whether you have a dependent child. Once you've run through the questions, the software suggests an answer—for example, "your filing status is head of household."

TABLE 2.1 Tax Return Preparation Software

PRODUCT	EASE OF USE	COST*	INTE-GRATION	BREADTH OF COVERAGE	HELP
TaxAct 2000 Deluxe** (2nd Story Software, Inc.) 800-373-3600 (www.taxact.com)	Interview format—seven-step approach—interview (including review and life events questions)	$9.95 (includes 1 federal e-file state forms $12.95, plus state e-file additional $4.95 but not available for all states)—standard version is free (doesn't include e-file)	Some	Standard	Moderate—limited (separate window for tax tips and general answers)
TaxCut Deluxe (Kiplinger) (www.taxcut.com)	Interview format—five step return completion approach; split screen shows interview plus forms	$19.95 (includes 1 federal e-file and rebate coupon for 1 state filing)	Import data from last year's TaxCut, TurboTax and TaxSaver, plus MIcrosoft Money and Quicken	Standard	Extensive
TurboTax** (Intuit) 800-335-1348 (www.intuit.com)	Interview/forms format; automatic uninstall option after return is filed	$29.95—state free with rebate (includes 1 federal and 1 state e-file through rebates)	Import data from last year's TaxCut, TurboTax, and TaxSaver, plus Microsoft Money and Quicken; retrieve W-2 and 1099 data from participating companies	Standard	Extensive—tax tips
TurboTax Deluxe (Intuit) 800-335-1348 (www.intuit.com)	Interview/forms format; automatic uninstall option after return is filed	$39.95—state free with rebate (includes 1 federal and 1 state	Import data from last year's TaxCut, TurboTax, and TaxSaver,	Standard	Extensive—tax tips, government instructions, IRS publications, video

(Continued)

TABLE 2.1 *(Continued)*

PRODUCT	EASE OF USE	COST*	INTE-GRATION	BREADTH OF COVERAGE	HELP
		e-file through rebates)	plus Microsoft Money and Quicken; retrieve W-2 and 1099 data from participating companies		library; paid live help available
Turbo Tax for Home and Business (for independent contractors and sole proprietors) (Intuit) 800-335-1348 (www.intuit.com)	Interview/ forms format; automatic uninstall option after return is filed	$???— state free with rebate (includes 1 federal and 1 state e-file through rebates)	Import data from last year's TaxCut, TurboTax, and TaxSaver, plus Microsoft Money and Quicken; retrieve W-2 and 1099 data from participating companies	Designed for the sole proprietor; can generate W-2s and 1099s	Extensive— tax tips, government instructions, IRS publications, video library; paid live help available

*Retail cost before promotions, rebates, and discounts that can lower these prices. Software may also include free *e-filing*.
**Comparable product for Macs.

IMPORTING LAST YEAR'S TAX INFORMATION.   If you used software to prepare your return last year, you can save yourself the time and effort of inputing your personal information—address, marital status, etc. (assuming nothing has changed)—by transferring last year's information to this year's return. With one keystroke you can automatically instruct your computer to pick up last year's data.

You can always import data from last year's return if you use the same (but updated) software this year. The software may also allow you to import last year's data from a different product. For example, TurboTax lets you import data not only from TurboTax but also from TaxSaver and TaxCut.

IMPORTING THIS YEAR'S FINANCIAL DATA.   Instead of inputing information about wages and other compensation from W-2 forms and invest-

Do It Better . . .

Importing last year's tax information gives you another check on the accuracy of your current tax return. By looking at income and deductions from the prior year you can make sure you don't overlook items for the current year. For example, if you reported interest income from Bank B last year, importing data from last year's return will prompt you to check on whether you received any interest from Bank B this year.

ment income from 1099s, you can have your computer do it for you—if your software provides this feature. As long as you have Internet access and the employer or financial institution is a participant in this information program, you can use your software to collect your necessary data online. For 2000 returns, the following companies were participants in Intuit's program for TurboTax and TurboTax for Mac:

- Ceridan.
- Cititrade.
- Fidelity Investments.
- INVESCO Funds.
- PeopleSoft MarketPlace.
- Salomon Smith Barney.
- T. Rowe Price.
- TD Waterhouse.

You can also import financial data from financial software you use throughout the year to pay your bills and keep track of expenses, investments, and other financial information—if your software sup-

Do It Better . . .

For 2001, check on participants in your software's information sharing program. As security issues are solved, an increasing number of participants are anticipated.

ports this function. For example, TurboTax lets you import data from its Quicken and QuickBook products as well as from other financial software such as MS Money.

NAVIGATING TAX SOFTWARE. Generally, you'll be asked a question. Once you respond—by clicking yes or no or entering the necessary information—you can proceed by clicking "next."

Forgot to enter something? Misentered something? You can retrace your steps by clicking "back" to revert to a prior screen. You may have to click several times if you want to go back several screens.

STAGES IN TAX PREPARATION. While each software product may label the processes of tax preparation differently, they all follow a basic approach:

- Enter preliminary information—your vitals (name, Social Security number, address, etc.). You may be able to import this information from last year's form to save you from re-entering this basic data.
- Enter your tax information—income items, deductible expenses, tax withholding, estimated tax payments, expenses for which a credit may be claimed, etc. You may be able to import some information—from W-2s or 1099s—if the payer participates in an online information program and your software can retrieve it.
- Tax computation—performed automatically for you to produce your final tax. This may be an overpayment that can be refunded to you or an underpayment of taxes you still owe.
- Review—a check of your return to make sure you haven't omitted information necessary for processing. For example, if you filed Schedule B to report interest and dividends, you must check the boxes—yes or no—in Part III of Schedule B relating to foreign bank accounts and trusts. The software will tell you what's missing and provide you with an opportunity to fill in the blanks.

When you have finished, you can then repeat the review to make sure you picked up and resolved all the problems. You can opt to override anything that the program says is an error and let the infor-

> **Do It Better . . .**
>
> In your review process, be sure to look for audit flags that your program may point out. Also, if you itemize your deductions, you may want to compare your amounts to the national averages, if your program provides this information. While you may be entitled to claim amounts in excess of the averages, doing so can be an audit trigger you may want to think about.

mation remain as you intend, but be careful in doing so. You may be inviting an IRS review of your return by keeping the "error." It's probably better to ask an expert for help if you can't find support for your "error."

- Prepare your state income tax return if necessary. State income tax returns are discussed in Part 2 of this book.
- Ready the return for filing—print out a hard copy of the return for your records. Then follow the instructions to *e-file* or to mail in a paper return. Filing is explained in Chapter 3.

Preparing Returns Online

Online Return Preparation in General

If you have Internet access you can prepare and file your return in one step. Or you can prepare your return—in as many sessions as you need—and later file your return through the same web site. The cost of electronic preparation and filing generally runs between $10 to $70. However, for simple returns for taxpayers with modest income, the service may be free. And there's no cost *until* you file. So preparation of the return is essentially free—a charge, if any, is for filing electronically.

In selecting an online site, factors similar to those used in assessing software should be considered. For example, how much help can you get through the site and what's the cost to you. Additional factors to consider include:

- *Equipment requirements*—what type of computer equipment and Internet access you need for the software. For example, most online sites support both PC and Mac formats, but you generally need at least 32 MB RAM and Internet Explorer 4.0 or higher, Netscape Navigator 4.06 or higher, or AmericaOnline 4.0 or higher. In addition your browser may have to be set up to accept cookies, Java, and Java Script. Equipment requirements are detailed at the web site you're considering.

- *Loading speed*—how long does it take to load the site? Some, such as TurboTax for the Web and HD Vest Online, loaded very quickly, while Kiplinger TaxCut Online was a bit slower to load—although loading time depends on your Internet access. And this could change for 2001 return preparation.

- *User friendliness*—how easy is it to figure out how to navigate the site to best complete your return. Most sites are very user friendly so this generally isn't an issue, but you need to check out what works best for you.

- *State taxes*—does the site support your state tax return? See Chapter 6 for details.

Table 2.2 lists many available tax preparation sites. Keep in mind that it is based on what was available for 2000 returns and doesn't necessarily include every site.

How to Prepare Your Return Online

Just like a manually prepared return, you need to gather all the tax information you'll need. This information includes:

- W-2 forms from all employers.
- 1099s that report interest, dividends, capital gain distributions, payments to independent contractors, royalties, gambling winnings, and state tax refunds.
- 1098s showing expenses you have paid for mortgage interest (property tax information may also be included), college tuition, etc.

Do It Better . . .

Since there's no cost for trying a site (you only pay when you file your return after you've completed it), you can take a test run at any site you're considering. Then stick with the one you like best—can use the easiest and get the most help.

TABLE 2.2 Online Tax Preparation Sites

SITE	WHO CAN USE IT	COST*
CompleteTax (www.completetax.com)	No income or complexity restrictions	$12.50 for completing and filing federal and state returns
esmartTax.com (www.eSmartTax.com)	No income or complexity restrictions	Preparation free; $5 *e-file* for Form 1040EZ; $10 *e-file* for Form 1040
FileYourTaxes (www.fileyourtaxes.com)	None	$14 *e-file* federal; $14 *e-file* state; $3 add'l forms and schedules
ezTaxReturn.com (www.eztaxreturn.com)	None	$24.95 for *e-file*
H.D. Vest (www.myhdvest.com)	No income or complexity restrictions	Free
H&R Block Tax Cut (www.taxcut.com)	No restrictions	$19.95 (state *e-file* is free)
Kiplinger TaxCut Online (www.taxcut.com)	No restrictions	Free for those who use Form 1040EZ; $9.95 for federal returns, $4.95 for state returns
Quick-Tax.com (www.quick-tax.com)	Form 1040EZ or Form 1040A only	$9.95
TaxACTonline.com (www.taxactonline.com)	No restrictions	For those who use Form 1040EZ $7.95 *e-filing* fee for a federal plus $7.95 state return; for others $9.95 for one federal *e-file* ($12.95 for state *e-file*)
TaxBrain.com (www.taxbrain.com)	Basic returns	$24.95 for preparing and filing federal and state returns
TurboTax for the Web (www.quicken.com/freedom)	No restrictions	Free for those with AGI** up to $25,000; free for those who use Form 1040EZ; $9.95 for federal returns, $9.95 for state returns (rebates for Quicken users)

*Reflects costs for 2000 returns.
**AGI is adjusted gross income—the amount reported for 2000 on line 4 of Form 1040EZ, line 19 of Form 1040A, or line 33 of Form 1040.

- Receipts for unreimbursed medical expenses, acknowledgments for charitable contributions, travel and entertainment logs or diaries for employee business expenses, and canceled checks or receipts for other deductible items.

- Last year's tax return to remind you of any carryover information—for example, capital losses, investment interest, passive activity losses, net operating losses, and home office deduction carryovers.

Log onto the site you want to use. You need to register at the site you've selected, providing it with your name, e-mail address and other information. Since the site contains your personal information, you must set up a password to access your return. Select a password and make note of it, storing it someplace you can find if you forget what it is—keep the password information with your tax records.

Prepare your return by responding to the questions posed at the site. Online sites use the interview format for tax return preparation. The process is easy—just click on yes/no responses where appropriate or fill in dollar amounts. The step-by-step process ensures that all income is reported and all deductions and/or credits can be claimed. Like return preparation software, online sites display a running total of your tax—what's owed or the refund due you.

If you want to stop midway through your return and pick up the process at another time, you can do so by saving the information you've already inputed. The information is stored for you and you access it by logging on—you don't have to reregister—just enter your password for access.

The time it takes to prepare a return varies greatly with the complexity of the return and your typing skills. However, if your return is relatively simple—you didn't make numerous stock trades during the year—you can probably finish it in under an hour.

Do It Better . . .

Assemble all the information you'll need to prepare your return *before* you log onto the tax return preparation site if you pay for your time online.

> ## Do It Better . . .
>
> Run a review or check of the return through the site if you have this option.
> This will ensure that any errors are detected so you can make corrections. It
> may also point out write-offs you've overlooked or show audit-triggers on your
> return—allowing you to make changes if you want.

Once you've completed your return, be sure to print out a hard copy for your files. You'll want this return so you can review it offline—checking for omissions and, yes, possible errors. You'll also want this return for your records—so you can refer to it next year. And you'll have a hard copy if you apply for a mortgage or other loan that requires the borrower's prior tax returns.

When you're absolutely sure that the return is ready for filing—go for it. *E-filing* is explained in Chapter 3.

Returns by Telephone

You don't need a computer—or even a handheld calculator—to figure out your taxes, complete your return, and even file it with the IRS. All you need is a TouchTone phone—preferably *not* a cellular or cordless phone—and certain key information explained below. This combined federal tax return preparation and filing method is called *TeleFile*.

ELIGIBILITY.   You can use this tax return preparation/filing method *only* if you receive a TeleFile tax package in the mail *and* you meet *all* of the following requirements:

- Your address is the same as it appears on the TeleFile printed address.
- You are single or married filing jointly and have no dependents.
- Your only income is from wages, salary, tips, taxable scholarships or fellowships, unemployment compensation, interest income of less than $400, Alaska Permanent Fund Dividends for Alaska residents, and qualified state tuition program earnings on distributions taken from the program.
- Your total income is under $50,000.

You can't use TeleFile if you didn't receive a TeleFile package, even if you meet all of the criteria above. The IRS selects who it will send the TeleFile package to based on tax filings of the prior year.

TeleFile enables you to claim an earned income credit if you're eligible to do so. But if you received any of the earned income credit in advance—through payroll adjustments—then you can't use TeleFile.

TeleFile lets you report wages and tax withholding from up to 10 W-2 forms. If you had more than 10 such forms, you can't use TeleFile.

Also, you can't use TeleFile if any of your personal information—filing status, name or address—has changed from what's printed on your TeleFile package. TeleFile is also barred from someone who has died—so, for example, if you're filing a return for a deceased parent who received a TeleFile package for the year, you can't complete and file the parent's final income tax return using this preparation/filing method.

TAX PREPARATION AND FILING. This is combined into one step under TeleFile. You key into the phone's Touch-Tone pad the information requested by a recorded message from the IRS. To complete this process, follow these simple steps:

STEP 1: Complete lines A–H of the TeleFile Tax Record. This is the information you'll be asked to key into your phone. Completing the record saves you from scrambling for information once you're on the IRS phone line.

STEP 2: Call the 800 telephone number provided in your TeleFile booklet.

CAUTION

If you key in any of this information incorrectly, you won't be able to proceed. Repeat the process so that your information matches what the IRS has listed for you in the TeleFile package.

STEP 3: Enter your information in response to each question. This information includes:

- Your Social Security number (and that of your spouse if you're married and filing jointly).
- The five-digit Customer Service Number (CSN) in your TeleFile tax package.
- Your date of birth.

STEP 4: Enter your wages, federal income tax withheld, and the employer identification number

---

Do It Better . . .

Listen to TeleFile's repetition of your entries. If you erroneously entered any information—what TeleFile has repeated—you can re-enter the information at that time. If you experience any technical difficulties, call the IRS at 800-829-1040. It may be the result of the phone you're using.

---

from each W-2 form. You can repeat this process for up to 10 W-2 forms. If you had more than 10 W-2 forms, you can't use TeleFile. Then enter any other income that you are asked about (refer to the eligibility checklist above). The IRS then computes your adjusted gross income, taxable income, and tax liability for you.

STEP 5: Enter again your CSN after hearing a statement—called a jurat statement—about penalties of perjury. On a joint return, this statement is repeated so a spouse can key in his/her separate CSN. The CSN is the equivalent of your written signature, agreeing that the information you've provided is correct and complete to the best of your knowledge.

CAUTION

If you do not receive a 10-digit confirmation number, your return has not been filed. You must repeat all of the steps and make sure that Step 6 has been met.

STEP 6: Write down the 10-digit confirmation number you'll receive over the phone on your TeleFile Tax Record. This tax record, combined with the confirmation number, serves as a "copy" of your tax return *and* proof of filing.

What happens *after* you complete and file your return through TeleFile—refund or payment and how to do it—is explained in Chapter 3.

Avoiding Common Mistakes in Online Return Preparation

Using computers, the Internet, and the TeleFile to complete your return virtually eliminates any math errors from your return—something that exists in more than 20% of hand-prepared returns. But math errors aren't the only mistakes found on returns. There are other mistakes you can make that will result in your paying too much—or too little—tax. Even worse, these mistakes may invite an IRS review of your return, which can lead to questions about other matters on your return.

Here is a listing of the more common mistakes found on returns—even those prepared with the latest technology.

ENTERING THE WRONG FILING STATUS. Usually your filing status is clear—for instance, you know whether you're married and filing a joint return. But sometimes filing status may be unclear. Remember that filing status for the entire year is determined by status on December 31st. For example, if you get married on December 31, 2001, you're considered married for all of 2001 and can file a joint return for the year. Complimentarily, if your divorce is finalized on December 31, 2001, you can't file a joint return for 2001 even though you were married for 364 days.

If you are unsure about your filing status, be sure to follow the interview format in software preparation to determine your status. The interview walks you through the points used to determine your status—for example, in determining head of household status, the software asks whether you have a dependent and whether you provided a household for the dependent.

OMITTING OR ENTERING THE WRONG SOCIAL SECURITY NUMBER (SSN) FOR EACH PERSON ON THE RETURN—filers and dependents. The SSN must match the number on file with the Social Security Administration.

An incorrect or missing SSN can have serious tax consequences. If a spouse's number is incorrect, the IRS may disallow the exemption claimed for that spouse.

If a dependent's SSN is incorrect or missing several adverse consequences result:

- No deduction will be allowed for the dependent.
- Head of household or surviving spouse filing status will be denied (only single will be permitted).

Do It Better . . .

If you've changed your name—through marriage or a legal name change—update your information with Social Security by filing Form SS-5, *Application for a Social Security Card*. For a form call the Social Security Administration at 800-772-1213 or click on www.ssagov. It takes about two weeks for the SSA to update its files to reflect the new information.

- No credits will be allowed for the child tax credit, the earned income credit, or the dependent care credit.

If your SSN fails to match up with interest and dividends reported to you on 1099's, you may become subject to backup withholding. This means that all interest and dividends you earn must have withholding taken from them at the fourth lowest individual tax rate (30.5% in 2001 and 30% in 2002) *before* payments are made or credited to you. While you can recoup the withholding when you file your return, you may be overpaying your taxes throughout the year, thereby making an interest-free loan to the government. For example, if your top tax rate in 2001 is only 27.5%, then being subject to backup withholding can easily create an overpayment.

FAILING TO ENTER INFORMATION EXACTLY AS IT APPEARS ON INFORMATION RETURNS. For example, if you receive bank interest of $403—the amount reported to both you and the IRS on Form 1099-INT—and you enter $304, the IRS computers will pick up this discrepancy and bill you for any taxes you may owe, as well as any interest and penalties, resulting from your error.

If you own stock or mutual funds jointly, so that only a portion of dividends reported on Form 1099-DIV belong to you, make sure you report this information correctly. If the 1099 is issued in your Social Security number, you need to report the *entire* dividend. In this case you are acting as a nominee for your co-owner. You then subtract the portion of the dividend belonging to

> **CAUTION**
>
> If you are a nominee for interest or dividends belonging to someone else, you must complete a Form 1099 and furnish it to that person by January 31, 2002. You must also give the IRS a copy of the form by February 28, 2002.

Did You Know?

Backup withholding on interest and dividends is required when the IRS notifies payers of these income items that Social Security numbers are missing or don't match up with those reported by payers. Banks, brokerage firms, corporations, and other payers then contact taxpayers to provide an opportunity to correct the problem. If you receive a "backup withholding" notice, respond immediately. Provide the correct information so that you won't be subject to backup withholding.

> ## Do It Better . . .
>
> Review your return carefully—regardless of which method you use. Make sure you've included all the information you need to and have entered that information correctly. Review the list of common errors and compare those with your return.

your co-owner. Your program should ask whether you are a "nominee" so it can walk you through this process. An adjustment must also be made for accrued interest on bonds you bought between interest dates.

MAKING WRONG ASSUMPTIONS. Just because you didn't itemize deductions last year is no reason to assume you won't be able to itemize on this year's return. Don't ignore the opportunity to test various filing strategies you may be entitled to use. The computer will perform "what if" calculations so you can see which alternative—for example, itemizing versus the standard deduction—results in the lower tax.

MISTREATING TAX ITEMS. Working with software or online is virtually—but not completely—foolproof when it comes to entering your tax information correctly. But you can still fool technology by mislabeling and then mistreating certain items. Examples:

- You can't turn nondeductible child support payments into deductible alimony simply by calling them alimony.
- You can't deduct a loss on the sale of your personal residence as a capital loss—it's a nondeductible personal loss.
- You can't deduct a contribution to a Roth IRA by calling it just an IRA—contributions to Roth IRAs are nondeductible.
- You can't deduct state estimated tax payments for 2001 that you made in January 2002—these become deductible on next year's return. But you can deduct 2000 estimated payments made in January 2001 on the 2001 return.

If you aren't sure about the tax treatment of a particular item, turn to the help features of your tax preparation materials.

Still not sure? Then log onto tax sites that can provide further guidance—they're discussed in Part 4 of this book and listed in the appendix. Still not satisfied? Your best bet now is to turn to a professional for assistance. You'll pay for the guidance you receive—but the help you get can save more than you'll pay in taxes or penalties you might otherwise be assessed.

CHAPTER 3

Filing Electronically

Once your return has been prepared it needs to be submitted to the IRS. You can, of course, mail in your return—even if you prepared it online or used computer software. But by mailing the return, you'll miss the opportunity to obtain the advantages offered by online filing—ease, accuracy, and quicker refunds.

Filing electronically is the wave of the future. Almost a third of taxpayers are already using *e-file* to submit returns and the government hopes that about 80% will do so by 2007. If you haven't yet used this filing method, consider doing so this year. If you've filed electronically in the past, you'll want to continue using this filing method. You can *e-file* regardless of whether you owe taxes or are due a refund. You can *e-file* whether you prepare your own return or use a paid preparer.

In this chapter you will learn about:

- Electronic filing alternatives.
- Mechanics of online filing.
- Getting refunds.
- Paying taxes owed.

Electronic Filing Alternatives

There are three ways you can file your return electronically: using your home computer, through an *e-file* provider, or with a telephone (if you are eligible to use this alternative). Regardless of which method you use, you no longer need to send in any paperwork after you've filed. *E-filing* can now be done entirely paperless—by using a self-select PIN number in place of your manual signature. In the past, you needed to send in a signature form as well as copies of your W-2 forms and any 1099s showing a payment of taxes, but if you use a self-select PIN you don't need to send in W-2s or other materials.

If you don't want to use a self-select PIN, you can still file electronically—but you must follow up the process by manually signing and then filing:

- Form 8453-OL, *U.S. Individual Income Tax Declaration for an IRS e-file On-Line Return*, if you use your personal computer to file your return electronically.

- Form 8453, *U.S. Individual Income Tax Declaration for e-file Return*, if you use a professional filer to file your return electronically.

There's no IRS fee for *e-filing*. However, you may have to pay a fee when using your home computer to file—generally only a few dollars. *E-file* providers charge a filing fee for their service—generally $35 to $50.

Creating Your Self-Select PIN

Instead of signing the return in ink you can use a special five-digit identification number as your electronic signature. You choose the PIN number—any combination other than all zeros. When filing a joint return, each spouse must choose a separate PIN number. If you had a self-select PIN when you filed your 2000 return, you can use the same number for your 2001 return—or you can choose a new number for the 2001 return.

You choose the number whether you file your own return or use a professional. You don't have to call or register the number with the IRS.

Don't worry if someone else chooses the same PIN number as you—your other tax information and date of birth are different and together will clearly identify you as the filer.

WHO CANNOT USE A SELF-SELECT PIN? Certain taxpayers cannot use an electronic signature. This doesn't mean they can't file electronically—merely that they must send in a manual signature form (listed above). Taxpayers in this category include:

- Under age 16 on December 31, 2001, who did not file a tax return for 2000.

- Require attachments to the return (other than Forms W-2, W-2G, or 1099-R). These include Form 2120, *Multiple Support Declaration* (when claiming an exemption for a dependent) Form 3113, *Application for a Change in Accounting Method*, Form 3468, *Investment Credit* (when claiming a credit for the rehabilitation of historic structures), Form 8283, *Non-Cash Charitable Contributions* (if required to complete Part B on appraisals for property donations exceeding $5,000), Form 8332, *Release of Claim to Exemption for Children of Divorced or Separated Parents*.

- Have a Social Security card marked "Not Valid for Employment."

- Filed in 2000 any of the following: Forms 1040-NR, 1040-PR, or 1040-SS.

- Died in 2001 and filing a final return.

Filing Electronically with Your Home Computer

If you have the right equipment and the right information, you can file your return any time of the day or night, seven days a week, from the comfort of your home.

EQUIPMENT. To file electronically you need a personal computer and Internet access. You can *e-file* whether you use a PC or a Mac. You generally need at least 32 MB RAM for memory and Internet Explorer 4.0 or higher, Netscape Navigator 4.06 or higher, or AmericaOnline 4.0 or higher. In addition your browser may have to be set up to accept cookies, Java, and Java Script. Equipment requirements are detailed at the web site you're considering as your filing site.

You can purchase the software that allows you to prepare and file your return. You can download such software from the Internet or complete the return online and file it at the same site—no separate software purchase is required. Return preparation is discussed in Chapter 2.

Did You Know?

If you prepare your return online, you don't pay for this service—until you file your return. For example, if you use TaxAct Online, you pay—$7.95 per form—when you *e-file* and not before then.

Generally, the software lets you *e-file* up to five returns (although only the first return may be included for free). This means that you can prepare returns for your children or other family members or even friends with a single program.

The software then converts the file for your return into a format that meets IRS specifications so it can be transmitted to the IRS.

INFORMATION NECESSARY FOR *E-FILING*. To file a paperless return you need to create a personal identification number (PIN) to identify you and act as your signature. You also need the following information:

- **Your adjusted gross income from last year.** If you didn't file a return in 2000, enter "0." If you were single in 2000 but married in 2001, each spouse uses the figure on the individual 2000 return. If you were married in 2000 and filed jointly but are single in 2001, use the joint return amount from 2000 as your adjusted gross income. Table 3.1 will help you locate your adjusted gross income.

- **Your total tax from last year.** If you didn't file a return in 2000, enter "0." If you were single in 2000 but married in 2001, each spouse uses the figure on the individual 2000 return. If you were married in 2000 and filed jointly but are single in 2001, use the joint return amount from 2000 as your total tax. Table 3.2 will help you locate your total tax.

- Your date of birth.

TABLE 3.1 Your 2000 Adjusted Gross Income

RETURN YOU FILED IN 2000—	LINE FROM THE 2000 RETURN—
Form 1040	Line 33
Form 1040A	Line 18
Form 1040EZ	Line 4
TeleFile Tax Record	Line 1

TABLE 3.2 Your 2000 Total Tax

RETURN YOU FILED IN 2000—	LINE FROM THE 2000 RETURN—
Form 1040	Line 56
Form 1040A	Line 34
Form 1040EZ	Line 10
TeleFile Tax Record	Line K

Filing Through an E-File *Provider*

Certain tax professionals have enrolled in the IRS's *e-file* program to become an *e-file* provider. You'll know that you're dealing with an authorized *e-filer* if they display the "Authorized IRS *e-file* Provider" sign (See Figure 3.1).

E-file providers are technically called Electronic Return Originators (EROs) because they are the parties that transmit tax return information to the IRS. A return preparer may or may not be an ERO—but the preparer who is not an *e-file* provider typically works with an ERO and so is capable of *e-filing* your return.

CAUTION

If you amended your 2000 return, be sure to use your *original* adjusted gross income and taxable income for electronic filing purposes in 2001. Don't use the amended information when filing your return electronically in 2001.

You can use an *e-file* provider in two instances—when the professional prepares and then files your return and when you prepare your own return but turn to a professional for filing it. If the professional prepares and *e-files* your return, you'll probably pay a single fee to cover both the cost of preparation and filing. If you use the professional *only* to *e-file* your return, you'll pay a filing fee—typically ranging from about $35 to $50 per return.

Do it Better . . .

Can't find your 2000 return? You can obtain your adjusted gross income and total tax by calling the IRS at 800-829-1040. You'll need to give the Customer Service Representative certain information—your name, Social Security number and current address—to verify that it's you who is requesting your personal tax information. Alternatively, you can ask the representative to send you a free transcript of your 2000 return—it takes about a week to 10 days.

FIGURE 3.1   Authorized *e-file* provider logo.

FINDING AN *E-FILE* PROVIDER.   If you prepare your own return and want a professional to file it—for example, if you don't have Internet access—find someone in your area who is authorized by the IRS to do this. If you don't know an *e-file* provider in your area you can locate one through a search at the IRS web site (www.irs.gov/elec_svs/ss-pin.html). Enter your zip code and you'll see a listing of *e-file* providers in your area.

FREE *E-FILE* PROVIDERS.   Taxpayers who are seniors (age 60 or older) or have low- to-moderate income may be eligible for free tax return preparation and *e-filing*. Only Forms 1040, 1040A, 1040EZ, and Schedules A and B can be filed through these free providers. Volunteers act as preparers and then file returns electronically under one of the following programs:

Do It Better . . .

When shopping for an *e-file* provider, be sure to get the price for *e-filing* both a federal and state return (if required). Since all *e-filers* must meet IRS standards, if you self-prepare your return then you generally should select the *e-filer* with the lowest cost.

Do It Better . . .

If you don't know which provider to select, consider using one that's been endorsed by the IRS. You can see a listing of *e-file* providers recognized by the IRS as exemplary by clicking on the Exemplary EROs at www.irs.gov/elec_svs/ss-pin.html.

- Volunteer Income Tax Assistance (VITA) Program.
- Tax Counseling for the Elderly (TCE) Program.

To find a VITA program, call the IRS at 800-829-1040. To find a TCE program, contact the American Association of Retired Persons (AARP) at 888-227-7669 or click on www.aarp.org/taxaide.

Using Your Telephone to File

You may be eligible to use TeleFile—a system in which you complete your return and file the information in one easy process. You can use TeleFile whether you owe taxes or are owed a refund. Eligibility for TeleFile and the steps you take in completing your return are discussed in Chapter 2.

To file your return using TeleFile you simply complete the process as the telephone instructs you.

- Enter your self-select PIN number or Customer Service Number (CSN) on your TeleFile instruction booklet to verify that you've listened to the statement on the penalties for perjury (called a jurat statement). You don't have to manually sign the return or send in any paper signature form. If the return is a joint return, the taxable income amount, tax, and refund or balance due for the spouse will be stated so that the spouse can enter the self-select PIN or CSN.

- Record the 10-digit confirmation number given to you over the phone at the end of the filing process. Write the number in the space provided in your TeleFile Tax Record. This is your proof of filing.

> **CAUTION**
>
> Wait for the confirmation number before you hang up the phone. If you hang up before hearing the confirmation number, your return has *not* been filed, even if you've keyed in all the necessary information.

Did You Know?

The IRS estimates that it only takes about 10 minutes on the phone to complete your return and file it using TeleFile. But it may take you a few minutes longer to assemble the information and complete the TeleFile Tax Record you'll need for making the call.

If you owe taxes, follow the instructions later in this chapter on how to pay the outstanding amount. You have the same payment options with TeleFile as you do with *e-file*—check, credit card, or debit to your bank account. If you want to authorize a debt to your bank account, be sure to complete lines E through H of your Tele-File tax record. These lines record your bank account number, the bank's routing number, and the type of account the funds will be debited from.

Mechanics of Online Filing

Filing Electronically with Your Home Computer

E-filing is easy. All you need to do is assemble the information listed above and then follow the prompts from your software. Your software will ask whether you want to file electronically. Answer yes.

When you are satisfied that your return is complete and accurate, proceed to the filing steps in your software. Enter the information required to enable you to *e-file*—your 2000 adjusted gross income and taxable income, date of birth and self-select PIN—when prompted by your software program to do so.

The software converts your tax return into a format that's acceptable for filing. When you *e-file* from your home computer, you're not filing directly with the IRS. You are going through an electronic return transmitter—the software company or someone else—who submits the return on your behalf. The process is seamless—you do your part and the system does the rest to get your return to the IRS.

IF YOUR RETURN IS ACCEPTED.   The IRS will acknowledge that your return has been accepted. This transmission of acceptance is your proof that the return has been filed—and accepted. It generally takes about 48 hours from the time of transmission to receive an acknowledgment.

IF YOUR RETURN IS REJECTED.   If there is a problem with your return—information is missing or incorrect—the return will be rejected. You'll be given a customer support number that you can call for help in correcting the problem. Once you correct it, you can resubmit the return.

One of the most common reasons that a return is rejected is because you (or your spouse's) name doesn't match the Social Security

Do It Better . . .

Even though *e-filing* is instantaneous, don't wait until the last minute to file your return. It may be rejected and you'll have to refile. It's better to *e-file* the return at least a couple of days prior to the filing deadline so you'll be sure to receive an acknowledgment by the deadline.

number recognized by the Social Security Administration (SSA). This can occur when a person marries or divorces during the year and changes his or her name. In this event, you have two choices:

- Change the name on the return to agree with the SSA's number.
- Change the name with SSA. You can do this by calling 800-772-1213 or click on www.ssa.gov. You'll have to wait about two weeks for the SSA to update its files so that the IRS can recognize the match for the name and Social Security number. If there's less than two weeks before the filing deadline, you'll need a filing extension. Otherwise you'll have to file a paper return.

If you believe the information on the return is correct, even though the IRS has rejected the return for incorrect information—for example, the IRS says your dependent's Social Security number is incorrect but you know it's correct—you'll have to file a paper return. There's nothing you can do electronically to change the situation and attempting to refile electronically will only produce the same rejection and delay the filing of the return. When you file the paper return, attach an explanation supporting your claim—for example, a photocopy of your dependent's Social Security card.

Other situations in which you may have to file a paper return—there's no way to fix the return for refiling—include:

- When your primary Social Security number was previously used as a dependent's Social Security number—the IRS has already received for the year a return claiming a taxpayer as a dependent, and now a second return is showing that same Social Security number as that of the taxpayer who's filing the return but there's no indication on the return that the filer is claimed as another taxpayer's dependent.

- When a dependent's Social Security number was used as the primary taxpayer's number and claimed self as an exemption on another return—this is the flip side to the situation above. Here the so-called dependent's return is filed first and then the return claiming the dependency exemption is filed.

- When the Social Security number listed on the return does not match the date of birth on file with SSA.

The fact that the error message says that your Social Security number has already been used on another return doesn't necessarily mean that someone has stolen your identity. It simply means that the SSA number has possibly been misused on another return—for example, to claim a dependency exemption. However, if this problem arises, you must file a paper return for this year. You can't correct the problem and refile.

> **CAUTION**
>
> **If your return is rejected with a message that your Social Security number has already been used on another return filed for the year *and* you believe you may be the victim of identity theft or tax fraud, you can make an anonymous report by calling the IRS at 800-829-0433.**

Filing through an E-File *Provider*

Whether you prepare your return yourself or use a tax professional to prepare your return, the professional can file your return electronically for you. You can use an *e-file* provider if you don't have Internet access. The *e-file* provider generally charges a fee for this service—up to about $50 per return. Be sure to ask for the cost up front if you want to comparison shop for *e-file* providers.

Your *e-file* provider will use your self-select PIN to file your return. To enable the provider to so this, you must manually sign an *e-file* signature authorization. This will allow the provider to file your return anytime—you won't have to be present for filing.

Instead of using a self-select PIN, you can manually sign Form 8453, *U.S. Individual Income Tax Declaration for an IRS e-file Re-*

> **Did You Know?**
>
> Professionals who file your returns electronically go by several names. They're called *e-file* providers. They're also called EROs—electronic return originators.

turn. This authorizes the ERO to file your return and acts as your return signature.

The ERO will forward your electronically formatted return to the IRS for processing. The IRS then checks your return for errors and missing information that prevent acceptance of your return. If the IRS cannot process your return, it is sent back to the ERO for correction or clarification. The ERO can then resubmit the return.

Once the IRS accepts the return, it sends an acknowledgment to the ERO. This is your proof of filing. Again, it generally takes about 48 hours from the time of transmission to receive the acknowledgment.

Getting Refunds

If the government owes you a refund because you overpaid your taxes you have several choices of what to do:

- Have the government mail a check to you for the refund amount.
- Have the refund—all or part—credited to your estimated taxes for 2002.
- Have the refund deposited directly into your banking account.

If you received a refund last year and opted for one of these alternatives, you don't have to use the same refund method this year. You can choose whichever method best suits your situation now.

NOTE

Your decision to apply part or all of your refund toward your 2002 cannot be changed after your return is filed. This choice is irrevocable.

REFUND BY MAIL. Refunds by mail take about three weeks—depending on when you file your return (it can be a little longer if you file around April 15th). To receive a refund check you don't need to take any action. Simply by *not* directing that the refund be credited to next year's estimated taxes or by completing the direct deposit in-

Do It Better . . .

Want to see what you can expect in the way of a refund before you actually prepare your return? You can work your way through a two-minute online refund estimator at www.securetax.com/estimator.asp.

Do It Better . . .

If you move after you file your return, be sure to notify the IRS of a change of address so your refund check can find you. You can download file Form 8822, *Change of Address*, from the IRS web site. The IRS notes that in 2001 it was still holding refund checks totaling more than $67.4 million because taxpayers couldn't be located.

---

formation, the government will automatically issue a refund check to you.

CREDIT TO ESTIMATED TAXES. If you want all or part of your refund of 2001 taxes applied to your 2002 estimated taxes, you must indicate the dollar amount on the appropriate line on your tax return.

If you file a joint return, the refund is automatically credited to the first Social Security number listed on the return. If you want it credited to the account of the spouse listed second, you must send a separate statement to this effect. Once you direct the credit to the spouse listed second it cannot be changed.

CAUTION

The IRS is not responsible for a lost or misdirected refund deposit. For example, some institutions will not deposit a joint check into an individual account. So make sure that the institution will accept the direct deposit and that the information you provide for routing your deposit is correct.

DIRECT DEPOSIT. Unless you opt to apply some or all of your return toward next year's estimated taxes, using direct deposit is the best way to receive your money. You get your refund fast—refunds via direct deposit take about two weeks (compared to three weeks or more with refunds by mail, depending on the time of the year you file). This payment method is more secure than refunds through the mail. In the 2000 tax year, about one-third of those receiving refunds opted for this method of receipt. You avoid the need to make a bank deposit—often requiring a trip to the bank.

To use direct deposit you simply complete the direct deposit information on your return. (See Figure 3.2.) This information includes the name of the bank or other financial institution (such as a brokerage firm or mutual fund) to which you want to direct the payment. By providing

Refund	66	If line 65 is more than line 57, subtract line 57 from line 65. This is the amount you **overpaid**	66	
Direct deposit? See page 50 and fill in 67b, 67c, and 67d.	67a	Amount of line 66 you want **refunded to you** . . . . ▶	67a	
	▶ b	Routing number	▶ c Type: ☐ Checking ☐ Savings	
	▶ d	Account number		
	68	Amount of line 66 you want **applied to your 2002 estimated tax** ▶	68	
Amount You Owe	69	**Amount you owe.** Subtract line 65 from line 57. For details on how to pay, see page 51 ▶	69	
	70	Estimated tax penalty. Also include on line 69	70	

FIGURE 3.2 1040 refund section on the 2000 return.

this information, the government knows *not* to mail your refund check but deposit it directly. You must include:

- The routing number. This is a nine-digit number that you'll find on the front of your checks from the bank or financial institution. You'll see this number on the lower left side of the checks. The first two numbers *must* be 01 through 12, or 21 through 32—any other number and the direct deposit won't work. Unsure of your routing number? Ask your bank or other financial institution to provide it for you.

- Type of account. Check off whether the deposit will be made to a checking or savings account.

- Account number. This is a combination of numbers and letters of up to 17 characters that appears on the bottom of your check to the right of the routing number. Include hyphens but do not include spaces or other characters. Enter the number starting to the extreme left. If your account number has less than 17 characters, leave the unused boxes blank. Do not confuse the account number on the bottom of the check with the check number that appears in the upper right corner of the check and to the right of the account number on the bottom of the check.

Do It Better . . .

If you received a refund, don't congratulate yourself. You've merely made an interest-free loan to the government. Take this opportunity to reaccess your withholding and/or estimated tax payments so that you can more closely approximate your tax liability for 2002.

Paying Taxes Owed

If you have underpaid your taxes and owe the government money, you can pay your taxes in one of three ways:

- Debit from your checking or savings account.
- Credit card.
- Mailing a check or money order. Make the check payable to the United States Treasury—not to the IRS. Be sure to enter your Social Security number on the front of the check (on a joint return enter the first Social Security number that appears on the form) and the name of the return you're filing—for example, "2001 Form 1040." Include Form 1040-V, *Payment Voucher*, with your check to ensure that the check is properly credited to your tax account. Do not staple or otherwise attach the payment to the voucher—merely include both in an envelope and mail the payment to the address included in the instructions to the return. Software will automatically provide you with this information when you print out the return.

Using either of the first two payment methods gives you an immediate acknowledgment that your payment has been accepted.

DIRECT DEBIT.　You can authorize the government to debit your checking or savings account for the amount of taxes due. You make this authorization by providing the information on your return.

You must include your bank routing information and account number as explained earlier in this chapter.

You can specify the exact date you wish to have the funds debited from your account—it need not be the same day you file your return. For example, you can *e-file* your return on March 1, 2002, while directing that the Department of the Treasury debit your checking account on April 15, 2002.

CREDIT CARD.　You can charge your tax balance to your Discover Card, American Express Card, or MasterCard. Currently, VISA does not participate in the tax payment program.

You can authorize payment on any date you select—it need not be the same date you file your return. For example, you may *e-file* your return on April 1, 2002, but authorize a credit card payment on April

Did You Know?

It can take up to 7 days before the payment is posted to your credit card account. Don't assume that your authorized payment hasn't been made to the government if you check your credit line within 7 days of making the charge.

15, 2002. There is no tax-saving reason to authorize payment *before* the filing deadline.

Using a credit card is a convenient payment method. And it may entitle you to certain benefits such as frequent flyer miles through the credit card company. However, it can also be an expensive payment method. While the IRS doesn't charge any fee for this payment method, the commercial companies making the payment arrangement do. You are charged a 2.5% "convenience fee" for charging your taxes. So if your tax bill is $1,200, the convenience fee is $30 ($1,200 × 2.5%). Alternatively, you can inquire about the convenience fee at 800-2PAY-TAX for Official Payments Corporation or 877-851-9964 for PhoneCharge, Inc.

To authorize a payment by telephone or computer, call or click on either of the following:

- Official Payments Corporation at 800-2PAY-TAX or www.official payments.com.
- PhoneCharge, Inc. at 888-ALLTAXX or www.About1888ALL TAXX.com.

If you use QuickenTurboTax or TurboTax for Mac you can charge your taxes with Discover Card when you file electronically.

In addition to the convenience fee, you'll also owe interest according to the terms of your credit card company. Thus, if you don't immediately pay the balance due resulting from your tax payment, you'll owe interest on your credit card balance. And the IRS has stated that this interest isn't deductible—even if you itemize your deductions.

To make a payment, follow the prompts from the payment company. You'll be asked—by phone or online—to enter certain key information. After you have completed the transaction, you'll receive a payment confirmation number as your proof of payment. If you use ALLTAXX, you can receive a faxed confirmation number.

Do It Better . . .

Be sure to write down the payment confirmation number that you are given at the end of the transaction. Make note of this number on the upper left hand corner of your return that you keep as your copy. It's a good idea to note the amount of the authorized payment—the tax and the convenience fee.

If You Can't Pay Your Tax

If you are unable to pay the balance due using any of the above methods, don't let this stop you from filing your return on time. By filing on time you'll avoid penalties for late filing. And there are several options for arranging to pay your taxes that can minimize or avoid additional costs to you.

PAYING IN INSTALLMENTS.   If you believe you'll be able to pay your taxes if you just have a little more time but you want also to minimize any late payment charges by taking action, you can request an installment agreement. This agreement allows you to pay your balance over time.

Make the request by filing Form 9465, *Installment Agreement Request*, with your return. This form can be filed electronically. Generally, it takes the IRS about a month to respond to your request—a little longer if you file after March 31st.

There is a $43 fee for setting up the agreement. Don't send this fee with Form 9465—the IRS will roll this cost into the installment agreement.

Eligibility for an installment payment agreement depends upon the amount of tax outstanding and other factors. Use the following guidelines to see if you can qualify for an automatic installment payment agreement. You can also use an online interactive process to

Did You Know?

The IRS approves almost all requests for installment agreements if you can pay within 12 months and keep current on this year's taxes. For example, in 1999 62% of all proposed agreements were accepted.

make this determination and even to see what your monthly payments would be (www.irs.gov/ind_info/coll_stds/collect.html).

- *If you owe no more than $10,000.* You're automatically eligible to make installment payments (assuming certain conditions are met). You must pay all of the outstanding balance within three years.

- *If you owe more than $10,000 but not more than $25,000.* The IRS will generally consent to an agreement that allows you to spread payments over no more than five years. While this installment arrangement isn't automatic, you can request the agreement using streamlined procedures that do not involve the filing of any liens on your property.

- *If you owe more than $25,000.* The IRS *may* agree to an installment agreement if you make a request and have a valid reason for paying over time. In this situation, however, all terms are negotiable.

An installment agreement does not avoid penalties and interest charges on your late payments. The penalty for late payment under an installment agreement is 0.25% per month (which is half the usual rate). The interest rate on underpayments is adjusted quarterly. For the first quarter of 2001, the interest rate on underpayments for individual taxpayers is 9%; for the second quarter of 2001 the rate dropped to 8% and for the third quarter to 7%.

REQUEST A REDUCED PAYMENT. If you don't think additional time will enable you to fully satisfy your tax liability—for example, paying the tax would cause a severe or unusual economic hardship—ask for an offer in compromise to reduce the amount owed. Unlike installment agreements, offers in compromise are not automatic, no matter what

---

Do It Better . . .

Pay as much as you can when filing your return using the above payment methods. By doing so, you minimize interest and possible underpayment penalties. Then ask for the installment agreement for the balance of taxes owed.

the circumstances. But the IRS will negotiate with you because it reasons that collecting something is better than nothing. It can take several months before you have an answer to your request. During that time, you'll have to make some payments on the outstanding taxes due.

To be eligible for an offer in compromise that allows you to pay only pennies on the dollar, you generally must show some economic hardship.

Request an offer in compromise by sending Form 656, *Offer in Compromise*, to the IRS district director's office where your liability is pending (mail the form in triplicate). The form is *not* filed with your return. Assuming there's no question about the amount of the tax owed, you must include detailed financial information on Form 433-A (or 433-B if you're self-employed).

Propose the amount you think you can pay—either in a lump sum or installments. Explain the reasons why you believe the IRS should accept your offer—you don't have the money now and don't have any reasonable prospects of obtaining it in the future. Your assets and your income—now and in the future—are taken into account by the IRS in deciding whether to accept your offer or some variation on it.

To obtain an offer in compromise you must also agree to certain terms:

- Any refunds and overpayments in the future will be retained by the IRS.
- You waive the statute of limitations on assessment and collection of tax for the period when the offer is pending (and for one year after installment payments have been made).
- You won't contest the amount of the compromised liability.
- You'll file all forms and make required payments on time for at least five years after the offer is accepted.

Example

Economic hardships include:

- You're incapable of earning a living because of a long-term medical condition.
- Liquidation of your assets would render you unable to pay your basic living expenses.

If you want an offer in compromise, it's generally advisable to work with a tax professional who can help you present your case to the IRS. For online help, try such sites as the following:

- Selik Law (www.taxworkout.com).
- Federal Tax Resolution (www.federaltax resolution.com).

CAUTION

If you receive an offer in compromise and then default on what you've agreed to pay, you'll not only owe the entire liability but also penalties and accrued interest.

CHAPTER 4

Preparing and Filing Other Federal Tax Forms

Online filing opportunities aren't limited to individual income tax returns. You can also request a filing extension and make estimated tax payments online. Doing so is convenient and easy—using your home computer or a telephone. You can use this technology to make payments, avoiding the need to file certain returns.

In this chapter you'll learn about:

- Filing extensions
- Estimated taxes
- Other forms

Filing Extensions

Individual income tax returns are due on April 15th. If April 15th falls on a Saturday, Sunday, or legal holiday, then the filing deadline is the next business day. If you don't file on time, you're subject to a late filing penalty. The penalty is 5% of the tax not paid by the regular due date of the return for each month (or part of a month) that the return is late. The maximum penalty is 25%. If the return is more

Did You Know?

The IRS estimates that more than 8 million taxpayers obtained filing requests last year.

than 60 days late, the minimum penalty is the smaller of $100 or the balance shown on the return when it is eventually filed unless you have a good reason for not filing on time.

You can avoid the late filing penalty by obtaining an automatic four-month filing extension available simply by asking. You don't need a reason for requesting an extension. You don't even need to pay the taxes you think are due. All you have to do is request an extension.

You can obtain this filing extension in three ways:

- Mailing Form 4868, *Application for Automatic Extension of Time to File U.S. Individual Income Tax Return*, to the IRS.

- Filing the form (Form 4868) electronically. You can do this by completing the filled-in form (Form 4868) at the IRS web site and filing it online or having a tax professional submit the form for you.

- *E-filing* by phone. All you do is call a toll free number and follow the steps outlined below. **Caution:** You cannot use this extension method if you did not file a tax return for the prior year.

General Rules for the Filing Extension

You must request a filing extension no later than the due date of the return (for example, April 15th). This deadline applies no matter which method you use to make your extension request. This date applies even if you are traveling abroad. If you plan to be out of the country on April 15th you should make your request before you leave—or call from abroad to use the *e-file* by phone method.

You must make a good faith estimate of your tax liability for the year. This is the amount you expect to report as your total tax when you file your return, based on the information you have at the time you make your extension request. Your tax liability includes not only your regular tax but also any alternative minimum tax, self-employment tax, and employment taxes for household employees.

Your estimate doesn't have to be right—you may owe more or less than what you estimated on the filing request. But if the IRS believes you didn't make a good faith estimate—the estimate you include with your request is so out of line with your final tax liability as to be totally unreasonable—your filing request will be voided and you'll owe a late filing penalty in addition to any interest and late payment penalty.

If the amount you estimate to be your tax liability is less than what you've paid for the year, you can make a tax payment with your extension request. You aren't required to do so as a condition for obtaining the extension, but it can be a wise move as explained later in this chapter.

Methods for Obtaining the Filing Extension

There are three methods for obtaining a filing extension. Regardless of which method is used, the deadline for making the request remains the same. The method you select for the filing extension does not affect the way you file the return. For example, you can mail in your extension request and then file your return electronically—as long as you do so no later than October 15th. Conversely, you can use the phone to obtain a filing request while later mailing in your return.

MAILING IN THE FORM. You can download the extension form—Form 4868, *Application for Automatic Extension of Time to File U.S. Individual Income Tax Return*, from the IRS web site at www.irs.gov. (See Figure 4.1.) The 2001 version of the form (the 2000 version is reproduced here) must be mailed no later than the filing deadline (April 15th).

Alternatively, you can complete the return online using the filled-in-forms section of the IRS web site (www.irs.gov). Click on "Forms and Pubs" and then on "Filled-in forms." Once completed, just print it out for mailing.

The form is straightforward, requiring only that you estimate to the best of your ability the amount of tax you expect to owe. You also list the tax payments you've already made through withholding and estimated taxes. Then you subtract the tax payments from the estimated tax liability to arrive at a balance. This is all you *must* do to get the

▼ DETACH HERE ▼

Form **4868** Department of the Treasury Internal Revenue Service (99)	Application for Automatic Extension of Time To File U.S. Individual Income Tax Return For calendar year 2000, or other tax year beginning , 2000, ending , .	OMB No. 1545-0188 **2000**

Part I Identification

1 Your name(s) (see instructions)

Address (see instructions)

City, town or post office, state, and ZIP code

2 Your social security number | 3 Spouse's social security number

Part II Complete ONLY If Filing Gift/GST Tax Return

Caution: *Only for gift/GST tax extension! Checking box(es) may result in correspondence if Form 709 or 709-A is not filed.*

This form also extends the time for filing a gift or generation-skipping transfer (GST) tax return if you file a calendar (not fiscal) year income tax return. Enter your gift or GST tax payment(s) in Part IV and:

Check this box ▶ ☐ if **you** are requesting a **Gift or GST tax** return extension.

Check this box ▶ ☐ if **your spouse** is requesting a **Gift or GST tax** return extension.

For Privacy Act and Paperwork Reduction Act Notice, see page 4.

Part III Individual Income Tax

4 Total tax liability on your income tax return for 2000 $ _____

5 Total 2000 payments . . . . . _____

6 **Balance.** Subtract 5 from 4 . . . . . _____

Part IV Gift/GST Tax—If you are **not filing** a gift or GST tax return, go to Part V now. See the instructions.

7 Your gift or GST tax payment $ _____

8 **Your spouse's** gift/GST tax payment

Part V Total

9 **Total liability.** Add lines 6, 7, and 8 $ _____

10 Amount you are paying. . . . . ▶ _____

Confirmation Number

If you file electronically, you will receive a confirmation number telling you that your Form 4868 has been accepted. Enter the confirmation number here and keep it for your records . . . . . . ▶ _____

Cat. No. 13141W   Form **4868** (2000)

FIGURE 4.1   Application for Automatic Extension of Time to File.

extension. No signature is required on the form. You can choose to make an additional payment as explained later in this chapter.

You can also use the form to obtain an extension of time to file a gift tax and generation skipping transfer tax (GST) return, Form 709, *United States Gift (and Generation-Skipping Transfer) Tax Return*, or Form 709-A, *United States Short Form Gift Tax Return.*

The form contains the mailing instructions. It's advisable to mail the form using certified mail so you'll have proof of filing. You can also use an authorized private carrier if you are *not* making a payment. But you can't use a private carrier if you're making a payment since these carriers are not permitted to deliver to a post office box, and all tax payments are sent to a post office box.

CAUTION

If you are making a payment with your extension request, send them to the address listed in the first column of the instructions to the form. If you aren't making a payment, send the form to the IRS Service Center for your area listed in the second column of the instructions to the form. You can't use an authorized private carrier to send your request if you're making a payment.

FILING THE FORM ELECTRONICALLY. You can file the form electronically using your home computer or through an *e-file* provider. Since the form does not require any signature, you don't need a self-select PIN number (explained in Chapter 3). You simply follow the instructions for your software—the extension is part of the tax return preparation material on the software. You'll need last year's return to provide your adjusted gross income and total tax—items needed to verify that you're the person you claim you are. Don't remember where to locate last year's tax information? This is explained in Chapter 3.

You can make a payment with your electronically filed extension by check (mail the check to the address shown in the instructions to Form 4868), by direct debit to your bank account or by charging a payment to your credit card—using an authorized service provider. How to make payments is discussed later in this chapter as well as in Chapter 3.

If you obtain a filing extension electronically, be sure to enter your confirmation number from the IRS in the lower right hand corner of the form. This is your proof that the form you filed electronically has been accepted. Do not mail in Form 4868.

CALLING A TOLL FREE NUMBER. You can call 888-796-1074 to request a filing extension through an interactive voice response system. You can use this method whether you want to make a payment at the same time.

To use the telephone method, you must first complete the following lines of Form 4868:

- Line 2—Your Social Security number. If you're married and requesting a joint extension, you must also complete line 3 for your spouse's Social Security number.

- Line 4—Your total tax liability that you expect to show on your return for the year. This is only your best guess. The actual figure may differ on a final return.

- Line 5—Total tax payments you made for the year through withholding and/or estimated taxes.

Did You Know?

You can obtain an automatic filing extension simply by charging a tax payment to your credit card and having the payment credited toward Form 4868. For example, if you charge your tax online through Official Payments Corporation at www.officialpayments.com you simply click on "Form 4868" to indicate that this if the form you're making a payment for. There's no need to complete or submit a separate form.

You also need a copy of your income tax return from last year—you're going to be asked certain information from it to verify who you are.

At the end of the call you'll be given a 10-digit number that confirms your filing request has been accepted. Be sure to enter this number in the space provided on Form 4868. Keep a copy of this form as your proof of extension. If you *e-file* by phone, don't mail in Form 4868.

Making Additional Tax Payments with an Extension Request

You are not required, as a condition of receiving a filing extension, to make any payments. But be aware that a filing extension does *not* extend the time for making tax payments. If you don't pay by the regular filing date what you ultimately determine you owe, you'll owe interest on any late payments—interest runs from April 15th until the date your return is actually filed. You may also owe a late payment penalty.

If you wish to make a payment with your filing extension request, thereby avoiding paying interest and penalty, you can use one of three ways:

- Direct debit (automatic withdrawal) from your checking or savings account. This is explained below.

- Credit card—authorizing payment by phone or online. This too is explained below.

- Mailing a check or money order with the filing extension request. Make the check payable to the United States Treasury—not to the IRS. Be sure to enter your Social Security number on the front of the check (on a joint return enter the first Social Security number that appears on the form) and the name of the return you're filing—for example, "2001 Form 4868" or if you used the phone to obtain the extension "2001 TeleFile Form 4868."

Do It Better . . .

When making a filing extension, pay as much as you can of the tax you think you'll owe. This will minimize interest charges and may help to avoid a tax penalty.

Do not staple or otherwise attach the payment to the form—merely include both in an envelope and mail them to the address included in the instructions to the form. If you used Telefile for the extension request, only send in your check—don't mail in Form 4868.

Using either of the first two payment methods gives you an immediate acknowledgment that your payment has been accepted.

DIRECT DEBIT. You can authorize the government to debit your checking or savings account for the amount of the payment you want to make with your filing extension request. To authorize the automatic withdrawal, you must make the following declaration:

I authorize the U.S. Treasury and its designated Financial Agent to initiate an ACH debit (electronic withdrawal) entry to the financial institution account indicated for payment of my Federal taxes owed, and the financial institution to debit the entry to this account. This authorization is to remain in full force and effect until I notify the U.S. Treasury Financial Agent to terminate the authorization. To revoke a payment, I must contact the U.S. Treasury Financial Agent at 1-888-353-4537 no later than 2 business days prior to the payment (settlement) date. I also authorize the financial institutions involved in the processing of the electronic payment of taxes to receive confidential information necessary to answer inquiries and resolve issues related to the payment.

You must provide your bank routing information and account number as explained in Chapter 3.

You can specify the exact date you wish to have the funds debited from your account—it need not be the same day you file your extension request. For example, you can *e-file* your extension request on March 1, 2002, while directing that the Department of the Treasury debit your checking account on April 15, 2002.

CREDIT CARD. You can charge your tax balance to your Discover Card, American Express Card, or MasterCard as long as the payment is at least $1. Currently, VISA does not participate in the tax payment program.

You can authorize payment on any date you select—it need not be the same date you file your extension request. For example, you may *e-file* your extension request on April 1, 2002, but authorize a credit

Did You Know?

It can take up to 7 days before the payment is posted to your credit card account. Don't assume that your authorized payment hasn't been made to the government if you check your credit line within 7 days of making the charge.

card payment on April 15, 2002. There is no tax-saving reason to authorize payment *before* the filing deadline.

Using a credit card is a convenient payment method. And it may entitle you to certain benefits such as free telephone usage or other benefits offered through the credit card company. However, it can also be an expensive payment method. While the IRS doesn't charge any fee for this payment method, the commercial companies making the payment arrangement do.

As explained earlier, you are charged a 2.5% "convenience fee" for charging your taxes. So if your tax bill is $1,200, the convenience fee is $30 ($1,200 × 2.5%). You will be told the amount of the convenience fee during the transaction and can terminate the transaction at that time if you choose not to charge the payment. Alternatively, you can inquire about the convenience fee at 800-2PAY-TAX for Official Payments Corporation or 877-851-9964 for PhoneCharge, Inc.

To authorize a payment, you can call or click on either of the following:

- Official Payments Corporation at 800-2PAY-TAX or www.official payments.com.
- PhoneCharge, Inc. at 888-ALLTAXX (www.About1888ALLTAXX. com).

In addition to the convenience fee for charging the payment, you'll also owe interest according to the terms of the credit card company.

Do It Better . . .

Be sure to write down the payment confirmation number that you are given at the end of the transaction. Make note of this number on the upper left hand corner of the form that you keep as your copy. It's a good idea to note the amount of the authorized payment—the tax and the convenience fee.

To make a payment in lieu of filing Form 4868, follow the prompts from the payment company. You'll be asked—by phone or online—to enter certain key information. After you have completed the transaction, you'll receive a payment confirmation number as your proof of payment. If you use ALLTAXX, you can receive a faxed confirmation number.

CLAIMING CREDIT FOR PAYMENTS MADE WITH YOUR FILING EXTENSION REQUEST. If you make a payment at the time you request a filing extension—by check, credit card, or direct debit—be sure to include this amount as a tax payment when you ultimately file your return. Include your payment for 2001 on:

- Line 64 if you file Form 1040.
- Line 41 if you file Form 1040A.
- Line 9 if you file Form 1040EZ.

Additional Filing Extension

If you can't file your return by the extended due date—August 15th—you can request an additional time to file. This additional filing extension isn't automatic—you need to have a reason for the added time. You must submit your request for an additional extension of time to file by August 15th—the date that the automatic filing extension expires. If you are given this additional extension you have until October 15th to file your return.

> **CAUTION**
>
> Generally you must have submitted Form 4868 before you can ask for an additional extension. However, in the case of undue hardship, the IRS may waive this prerequisite.

To date, you cannot obtain this additional filing extension electronically or by phone. You must submit a paper form, Form 2688, *Application for Additional Extension of Time to File U.S. Individual Income Tax Return*. The form contains space for you to explain your reason for seeking an additional filing extension. Alternatively, you may send a letter of explanation. Either way, the request is mailed to the same IRS service center in which Form 4868 was mailed (or would have been mailed had the request not been made electronically or by phone).

Estimated Taxes

If withholding from wages, Social Security benefits, pensions, or other payments won't cover the taxes you'll owe, you may need to make estimated tax payments. If you don't, you can be subject to underpayment penalties. Making estimated tax payments has been simplified by online payment options.

General Rules for Estimated Taxes

Estimated taxes aren't a concern for everyone. But self-employed individuals, retirees, and others with income not subject to withholding should determine whether they need to make estimated tax payments—and how much.

ESTIMATED TAX REQUIREMENTS. Approximate what your tax liability will be for the year. Then subtract from the amount of payments you make through withholding on wages, pensions, Social Security benefits, gambling winnings, and other payments. Also, add in any overpayment of last year's tax that you had credited toward this year's estimated tax payments. If the difference is more than $1,000, think seriously about making estimated tax payments. Unless you meet a safe harbor explained below, you'll be subject to underpayment penalties on any underpayments exceeding $1,000. The penalties are effectively the IRS interest rate on underpayments—a rate that can be adjusted quarterly. For example, for the first quarter of 2001 (January 1st through March 31st), the IRS interest rate on outstanding underpayments was 9%, for the second quarter of 2001 (April 1st through June 30th), the IRS interest rate was 8% and for the third quarter of 2001 (July 1st through September 30th), it was 7%.

You need to make estimated tax payments in order to avoid penalties unless your payments meet a safe harbor—the payments equal at least 90% of the tax for the year or 100% of last year's tax.

However, if your adjusted gross income last year was over $100,000 ($75,000 if you were married and filed separately)—you are consid-

---

Did You Know?

In 2002, the prior year safe harbor for high-income taxpayers increases to 112% of 2001 tax. In 2003 and thereafter, the prior year safe harbor for high income taxes is fixed at 110% of prior year tax liability.

ered a "high-income taxpayer." In this case your estimated tax payments for 2001 must equal at least 90% of the tax for the year or 110% of last year's tax.

If your underpayment is more than $1,000 but you didn't have to file a return last year or had zero tax liability, you won't be subject to underpayment penalties for this year—even if you don't meet the 90%/100% (or 110%) safe harbors.

Estimated taxes must cover not only your regular tax but also:

- Alternative minimum tax.
- Self-employment tax.
- Employment taxes for household employees.

The Internet can help you figure out what your estimated tax payments should be in order to avoid penalties. You can use an online calculator for this purpose at SmartMoney.com (www.smart money.com/tax/capital/index/cfm?story=estimated).

WHEN TO MAKE PAYMENTS. Estimated tax payments are made four times a year—generally April 15th, June 15th, September 15th, and January 15th of the following year. However, you don't have to make the fourth payment on January 15th if you file your tax return by January 31st and pay the balance of any tax at that time.

Farmers and fishermen have different estimated tax requirements. Farmers only have to make one payment for the year—generally by January 15th of the following year. But they can avoid having to make even this one payment if they file their return by February 28th of the following year. This exception doesn't apply to gentlemen farmers or individuals who grow their own produce in their gardens. To qualify as a farmer, you must receive two-thirds of your gross income this year or last year from farming.

Do It Better . . .

In making estimated tax projections, be sure to factor in year-end capital gain distributions from mutual funds, year-end bonuses, and other unexpected income that can easily raise your taxes. Also, take into account new law changes that will take effect for the year for which estimated taxes are being made.

Fishermen do not have any estimated tax requirements. This exception doesn't apply to weekend sportsmen. To qualify as a fisherman, you must receive two-thirds of your gross income from fishing.

Methods for Paying Estimated Taxes

Estimated taxes are only a payment—you don't need to file any form showing the IRS how you figured what you owe. There are three ways to make estimated tax payments:

- Mailing Form 1040-ES vouchers.
- By telephone.
- By personal computer.

In deciding which method you select for making estimated tax payments, factor in the cost and convenience of each of the following.

> **CAUTION**
>
> You can't mail the payment using a designated private carrier because payment is directed to a post office box and private carriers can't deliver to post office boxes.

MAILING FORM 1040-ES VOUCHERS. Mail in Form 1040-ES, which is merely a payment voucher on which you indicate your name, Social Security number (and information on a spouse if making a joint payment), and the amount of the payment you're making. You send the voucher along with a check to the address indicated in the instructions to the form. Don't attach the voucher to the check—merely include both in the same envelope.

Mail the payment using certified mail to have proof of the date you mailed in the payment. The postage is your only cost in mailing in a payment by check.

BY TELEPHONE. All you do is authorize a credit card payment to be applied toward your estimated taxes. You don't need to file any form.

Authorization of payment can be made on Discover Card, American Express Card, or MasterCard. Currently, VISA does not participate in the tax payment program. To authorize a payment call either of the following:

- Official Payments Corporation at 800-2PAY-TAX.
- PhoneCharge, Inc. at 888-ALLTAXX.

Dial the toll-free number you select. Then provide the company with the information requested—your name, Social Security number, and the type and amount of payment you're making. You'll then be given a confirmation number—write it down as your record of having made the payment.

Paying by phone is convenient and easy—you can use the automated phone lines 24-hours a day—during permissible periods. The cost of making estimated payments by phone is the same as the cost explained earlier for making payments in lieu of filing Form 4868. Consider the convenience fee and interest charges you may incur.

BY PERSONAL COMPUTER. Similar to the telephone payment method, you merely click on the web site for one of two authorized companies to authorize a payment by any of the credit cards listed above under payment "by telephone":

- Official Payments Corporation at www.officialpayments.com.
- PhoneCharge, Inc. at www.About1888ALLTAXX.com.

You can divide payment among two credit cards. For example, if you want to make a $2,500 estimated tax payment, you can opt to charge $1,500 on Discover and $1,000 on MasterCard.

Like payment by phone, paying by computer is certainly a convenience, but there's a cost involved. The cost of making estimated payments by computer is the same as the cost explained earlier for making payments in lieu of filing Form 4868. In deciding whether to charge estimated tax payments, consider the convenience fee and interest charges you may incur.

Other Forms

Amended Returns

If you made a mistake on your return—you omitted income or failed to claim a write-off you're entitled to—you can file an amended return. Generally, you have three years from the due date of your return to submit an amended return. If you miss this deadline, you can't file an amended return. So if you discover you overpaid your taxes, you must file an amended return to claim a refund before this deadline.

When you prepare an amended return for a prior year, you must use the tax information for that year—you can't use the information in your current instruction booklet. You can obtain old tax forms and instructions from the IRS by calling 800-829-1040 or clicking on www.irs.gov.

As of yet, the ability to prepare and file amended returns online is limited. For example, if you prepared your original return online, you probably have to download it, so you can have the information needed to prepare an amended return online—a separate process. And not all sites currently support the preparation and filing of amended returns.

Other Forms

Individuals may have to file other types of forms and, in some cases, can do so online.

- Information returns in the 1099 series. If you are a nominee of interest income or dividends, you must file a copy with the IRS. If you file electronically, you gain an extra month for filing. Information returns and their filing deadlines are explained in Chapter 9.

- Qualified retirement plan returns. If you are self-employed and maintain a qualified plan—even for just yourself—with assets exceeding $100,000 at any time after 1993, then you must file an annual return for the plan. Retirement plan returns are also explained in Chapter 9.

Preparing and Filing Your State Income Tax Return

CHAPTER 5

Preparing Your State Return

All of the advantages of *e-filing* a federal income tax return apply with equal force to state income tax returns—the process is easy and convenient, you can receive refunds much quicker than filing by mail, and frankly, it's the direction in which taxes are headed.

The process of *e-filing* state income tax returns is identical to the federal process detailed in Part 1 of this book. There are, however, certain wrinkles unique to state returns.

In this chapter you'll learn about:

- Return preparation options for state returns.
- Selecting tax software for state returns.
- Using software for state returns.
- Preparing state returns online.
- State returns by telephone.
- Getting state tax information.

Return Preparation Options for State Returns

Like your federal income tax return, there are a number of ways in which you can prepare your state income tax return. Here are your five options:

- Paper return—the old-fashioned way of filling in a form—typically one that's mailed to you in a tax package from the state.

- Fill-in forms at the state web site—some forms are strictly fill-in while some fill-in forms can perform math calculations. Once completed, you can print out the form for signing and mailing.

- Online. Some states have their own online preparation and filing option. There is also Quicken's Tax Freedom Project for free online preparation and filing, restricted to those with adjusted gross income below a certain amount. And other commercial sites allow for state online preparation and filing.

- Off-the-shelf software. Commercial products let you prepare your return. Most (but not all) can then be filed electronically.

- By telephone. Many states have a TeleFile option for preparing and filing returns by phone. In some states, availability of this option is restrictive. A handful of states offer one-step preparation and filing for federal and state returns—one call does it all.

Selecting Tax Software for State Returns

Take time to consider your software selection. You need a product that will suit your needs and be easy to use. Table 5.1 is a listing of online and off-the-shelf software that were available for 2000 returns. It's a good idea to tour the product's web site for details (and perhaps take a free product demo) to learn what each one is about and whether it's right for you.

You probably wouldn't buy a shirt without checking the label and trying it on. The same holds true for your tax preparation software. You need to look at several factors when selecting software for preparing your state income tax return. These factors include:

- *Availability.* Not every state has approved all software options. Check which software is authorized for use in your state (see Chapter 6).

TABLE 5.1 Commercial Software and Web sites for State Income Tax Returns

PRODUCT NAME	COMPANY	WEB SITE	STATE ONLINE FILING
Complete Tax (online only)	CCH Inc.	www.completetax.com	KS, IA, HI, IN, MD, AL, GA, CA, PA, MS, LA, OR, MI, NY, WI, WV, UT, SC, OK, OH, NC, NE, MT, MA, ME, RI, KY, IL, ID, DE, CT, CO, AR, AZ, MN, NM, DC
FileYourTaxes.com	Atilla M. Taluy	www.FileYourTaxes.com	CA, NC
H&R Block Online	Block Financial Corporation	www.hrblock.com	none
Kiplinger Tax Cut	Block Financial Corporation	www.taxcut.com	AZ, MI, IN, NJ, GA, HI, MD, SC, CA, PA, IL, OR, NY, MN, ME, NC, MN, RI, UT, VA
MyHDVest	H.D. Vest Technology Services, Inc.	www.myhdvest.com	IA, MI
ON-LINE 1040A	On-Line Taxes, Inc.	www.quick-tax.com	CA, NY
TaxAct	2nd Story Software	www.taxact.com	AL, AZ, IN, GA, MN, NY, NC, IA, CA, PA, IL, VA
TaxBrain.com	Petz Enterprises	www.taxbrain.com	AL, AZ, KS, AR, MN, UT, IL, NJ, NY, OH, VA

(Continued)

TABLE 5.1 *(Continued)*

PRODUCT NAME	COMPANY	WEB SITE	STATE ONLINE FILING
Tax-Engine.com	Tax Works by Laser Systems	www.tax-engine.com	AL, KS, MN, RI, UT
TaxSlayer	RCS	www.taxslayer.com	AL, AR, CA, CT, DE, DC, GA, IN, IA, KS, KY, LA, MD, MS, MO, NE, NM, NY, NC, OH, PA, SC, IL, MI, NJ, WV, WI
Turbo Tax for the Web (online only) Turbo Tax Turbo Tax for Mac*	Intuit	www.turbotax.com	AZ, KS, IN, MD, AL, GA, SC, IA, CA, PA, MN, MS, RI, NC, LA, IL, OR, MI, NY, ID, AR, MN, DC, UT, VA

*TurboTax for Mac does not support all of these states.

- *Suitability.* You need to determine whether the software will prepare the type of return you need to file. For example, you may need software that supports a part-year resident or non-resident return or software that supports a complex state return.

- *Cost.* This is perhaps the greatest variable among software options. Prices vary greatly. Price does not necessarily equate with value or performance. A costly product may not perform as well as a less costly one. On the other hand, a costly product may be well worth it if it's easy to use and can support all the state forms and schedules you need.

- *Customer support.* If you have questions make sure you can get them answered. Some products require you to submit questions online—resulting in a delayed response.

Did You Know?

You can deduct the cost of software and *e-filing* as a miscellaneous itemized deduction to the extent that miscellaneous expenses exceed 2% of your adjusted gross income. If you pay for the software in 2002, you can deduct it on your 2002 return that you'll file in 2003. But if you buy the software before the end of 2001, you can deduct it on your 2001 return filed in 2002.

Using Software for State Returns

There are three types of software you can use to prepare state income tax returns:

- State-provided software at its web site (only a few states currently provide this option).
- Online software. You don't need to download the software—you merely use it online. Generally you don't pay for the use of the software—you pay when you *e-file* your return.
- Off-the-shelf software that you can use to prepare your return and then, in most cases, file it online from your home computer.

Generally, whichever product you select, you need to complete your federal return first. State returns largely depend on the information found in your federal return. In some cases, you may not need to add any information to complete your state return—the software automatically picks up the information from the federal return and applies it to your state return. In this case, state income tax return preparation is instantaneous. All you may need to add to your state return is county and school district information.

However, in some cases, the information on your federal return may differ from that on your state return. Examples of different treatment include:

- Claiming the standard deduction on your federal return while itemizing deductions on your state return.
- Claiming a dependent on a state return where the exemption was waived on the federal return (for example, where the exemption was waived to enable the child to claim a Hope or lifetime learning credit).

- Making adjustments for depreciation.

- Reporting income exempt on a federal return that may be taxable on a state return. For example, interest on municipal bonds may be taxable on a state return even though it was exempt from federal income tax. So if you live in New York and earn interest on a California bond, the interest is exempt from federal income tax but subject to New York state income tax.

- Excluding income that was taxable on a federal return that may be tax-free on a state return. Examples of income taxable on the federal return that may be excludable on the state return include, refunds of state and local income tax, interest on U.S. government obligations, and certain pension income.

- Claiming deductions unique to the state. Some states have their own deductions distinct from those allowed on the federal return. For instance, you may be able to claim a state income tax deduction for contributions to state qualified tuition plans (529 plans).

- Claiming credits unique to the state. Some states have their own tax credits. For example, New York has a special household credit—the amount of which depends on household income. However, some federal tax credits may *not* be claimed on the state return. For example, some states may not recognize the federal education credits.

- Deductible gifts to state-sponsored funds. On the federal income tax return you can designate that $3 of your tax money be applied toward the federal election campaign fund. This designation doesn't change your tax liability—it's not a write-off. But some states have created special funds that are tax deductible. For example, there may be funds for wildlife preservation, a missing and exploited children clearinghouse, Alzheimer's research, or some other worthy cause.

You don't necessarily have to do anything special to have your state return preparation software make the necessary adjustments. However, where information is missing, for example, whether you want to donate to a certain fund, the software will prompt you for a reply and complete your state return.

Preparing State Returns Online

The makers of TurboTax have a special online option called Quicken Tax Freedom Project (QTFP) (www.quicken.com/freedom). This allows you to prepare your federal and state returns online and file them for free. For 2000 returns, this option was open only to those with adjusted gross income of $25,000 or less. Some other commercial sites offer similar free filing options with income restrictions.

Some states offer their own free online preparation/filing option. The online preparation and filing system goes by different names in different states. For example, it may be called "I-filing," "Web-file," "Net-file," or some other name. The states that offered this option for 2000 returns included: Delaware, Idaho, Iowa, Louisiana, Maine, Maryland, Massachusetts, Missouri, New Jersey, New Mexico, Oklahoma, South Carolina, Vermont, and Virginia. This list may be expanded for the filing of 2001 returns.

If you don't qualify to use a free online option, you may still be able to prepare your return and file it through a commercial web site (explained earlier in this chapter).

State Returns by Telephone

Last year four states—Georgia, Indiana, Kentucky, and Oklahoma— allowed you to use TeleFile to complete your federal and state returns at the same time—one phone call to provide the information necessary to complete and file both returns. It is expected that this option will be expanded to other states for 2001 returns.

States that don't offer one-step filing may still offer the TeleFile option to prepare and file the return by telephone. Most states limit this filing option to those receiving a TeleFile booklet—those who file simple returns. But some states, such as Kansas, open this option to all state residents.

Generally all that's required is to complete a worksheet found in your state TeleFile booklet that was mailed to you. Then follow the TeleFile instructions for filing your return as explained in Chapter 6.

Getting State Tax Information

Each state has its own tax rules and procedures. Every state has its own web site at which you can obtain this important tax information. If you don't have Internet access at home, you can probably get on the Web at your local library or school. On the Internet you can find:

- Income tax forms and other tax forms and information.
- Filing deadlines.
- Extension information.
- E-filing options.

Some state web sites are better than others and some are easier to navigate than others—but all can provide you with essential information. Table 5.2 is a survey of web sites for state tax authorities—revenue agencies or departments.

TABLE 5.2 State Tax Authority Web Sites

STATE	WEB SITE
Alabama	www.ador.state.al.us
Alaska	www.revenue.state.ak.us/
Arizona	www.revenue.state.az.us/
Arkansas	www.state.ar.us/dfa
California	www.ftb.ca.gov
Colorado	www.revenue.state.co.us
Connecticut	www.drs.state.ct.us
Delaware	www.state.de.us/revenue
District of Columbia	www.dccfo.com
Florida	www.state.fl.us/
Georgia	www2.state.ga.us/departments/DOR
Hawaii	www.state.hi.us/tax/tax.html
Idaho	www.state.id.us.tax
Illinois	www.revenue.state.il.us
Indiana	www.in.gov/dor/
Iowa	www.state.ia.us/government/drf/

TABLE 5.2 *(Continued)*

STATE	WEB SITE
Kentucky	www.state.ky.us/
Louisiana	www.rev.state.la.us
Maine	http://janus.state.me.us/revenue
Maryland	www.marylandtaxes.com
Massachusetts	www. state.ma.us/tax.htm
Michigan	www.treas.state.mi.us
Minnesota	www.taxes.state.mn.us
Mississippi	www.mstc.state.ms.us
Missouri	www.dor.state.mo.us
Montana	www.state.mt.us/revenue/
Nebraska	www.nol.org/home/NDR
Nevada	www.state.nv.us
New Hampshire	www.state.nh.us
New Jersey	www.state.nj.us/treasury/taxation
New Mexico	www.state.nm.us/tax
New York	www.tax.state.ny.us
North Carolina	www.dor.state.nc.us
North Dakota	www.state.nd.us/taxdpt
Ohio	www.state.oh.us/tax
Oklahoma	www.oktax.state.ok.us/
Oregon	www.dor.state.or.us
Pennsylvania	www.revenue.state.pa.us
Rhode Island	www.dor.state.ri.us
South Carolina	www.dor.state.sc.us
South Dakota	www.state.sd.us/treasurer
Texas	www.window.state.tx.us
Tennessee	www.state.tn.us/revenue
Utah	www.tax.ex.state.ut.us
Vermont	www.state.vt.us/tax
Virginia	www.state.va.us/tax/tax.html
West Virginia	www.state.wv.us/taxrev/
Wisconsin	www.dor.state.wi.us
Wyoming	http://revenue.state.wy.us

TABLE 5.3 Sites for Surveys of State Taxes

SITE	WHAT YOU'LL FIND
Federation of Tax Administrators (www.taxadmin.org/fta/rate/tax_stru.html)	State tax rates and structures
Tax Foundation (www.taxfoundation.org/pr-statelocal00.html)	A comparison of state taxes

Other Ways to Find State Tax Information

Thinking of moving to another state? Certainly the taxes you'll face there are one factor to consider when deciding on a move. It can be a tedious process to check each state's web site separately for a listing of income tax and other state tax information. But there's an easier way to compare the taxes in various states—by using special sites designed for this purpose. (See Table 5.3).

CHAPTER 6

Filing State Returns Electronically

If you live in Alaska, Florida, Nevada, South Dakota, Texas, Washington, or Wyoming, you don't have to file any state income tax return—there is no state income tax in these states. New Hampshire and Tennessee have a tax only on certain income—interest and dividends.

But if you live anywhere else, you may have to file a state return. You may be liable not only for state income taxes but also for local income taxes as well. For example, in New York, local income taxes are levied on residents of New York City and Yonkers. You may even be required to file a state income tax return, even if you are exempt from federal income taxes.

And if you live or work in more than one state, you may have to file multiple returns—one for your state of residence and others for states in which you are considered a nonresident or part-year resident.

In this chapter you'll learn about:

- Electronic filing alternatives.
- Mechanics of online filing.
- Getting refunds.

- Paying taxes owed.
- State-by-state survey of filing options.

Electronic Filing Alternatives

Just like filing your federal income tax return, you have a number of options for filing your state income tax returns:

- TeleFile.
- *E-filing* directly at state sites.
- Joint federal and state *e-filing*.
- Using state fill-in forms to prepare a return for mailing.
- Preparing and filing online with a home computer.
- Filing through an *e-file* provider.

CAUTION

Check the time limits for using the various filing options. In some cases, an option may only be available through April 15th while a different filing option would need to be selected for a later filing.

Not every state offers all of these options. And the requirements for using different options vary considerably from state to state. The first thing to check is your state's filing options. Don't rely on your memory from last year—the filing options may have been expanded for this year. You'll find this information listed in the tax return booklet sent to you from your state. You'll also find this information later in this chapter.

Mechanics of Online Filing

Simultaneous Filing

The IRS and a number have states have joined together to create a one-step filing process. A taxpayer files a federal return and consents to share information with his/her state of residence. This automatically processes a state return at the same time.

E-FILING. You can file your federal and state return in one step. Both returns are filed electronically at the same time in one transmission. In addition to the District of Columbia, Table 6.1 lists the 37 states that participated in the one-step filing program for 2000 returns.

One-step or simultaneous filing can only be done if the federal return has not already been filed. In other words, you must decide *be-*

TABLE 6.1 States Participating in the One-Step Filing Program

Alabama	Montana
Arizona	Nebraska
Arkansas	New Jersey
Colorado	New Mexico
Connecticut	New York
Delaware	North Carolina
Georgia	North Dakota
Hawaii	Ohio
Idaho	Oklahoma
Illinois	Oregon
Indiana	Pennsylvania
Iowa	Rhode Island
Kansas	South Carolina
Kentucky	Utah
Louisiana	Vermont
Maryland	Virginia
Michigan	West Virginia
Mississippi	Wisconsin
Missouri	

fore you begin to complete your returns and file them which filing option you'll use.

FILING BY PHONE.   If you're eligible to TeleFile your federal return, you may be able to also file your state income tax return with the same phone call. Some states already offer this single-call filing option (and more are expected to offer this option in the future). (See Table 6.2.)

Separate Filing

E-FILING.   In many states you can use a home computer or *e-file* provider to submit your return electronically.

> **CAUTION**
>
> To use the single-call TeleFile method you must have received *both* the federal and state TeleFile packages. If you receive a TeleFile booklet from the IRS but didn't receive one from your state, you won't be able to use this filing method.

TABLE 6.2 States Participating in the One-Call TeleFile Program

Georgia	Kentucky
Indiana	Oklahoma

- *Free* e-filing. A few states offer their own *e-filing*—use their web site to prepare and file your state income tax return online at no cost. Many other states participate in a free *e-filing* option for those with adjusted gross income of $25,000 or less using Quicken Tax Freedom Program (QTFP) or another approved commercial web site.

- *Online preparation and filing.* You can use commercial web sites approved by your state to prepare and file your return online. The cost is modest—generally no charge applies until you complete and file your return. The approved sites vary from state to state so check which ones you can select from.

- *Preparation and filing with commercial software on a home computer.* Instead of downloading software or preparing the return online, you can buy commercial software to prepare your return on your home computer. When you have completed the return, you can file it online using the same program. You pay for the software (unless the price of the state software is included with the cost of the federal software)—the filing fee may be included in the price or there may be an additional online filing fee. Again, the approved software varies from state to state so check which ones you can select from.

- E-file *provider.* If you have your return prepared by a tax professional, it can be filed online.

Do It Better . . .

To find an *e-file* provider in your area, check your state's web site. Many web sites list tax professionals by zip code or city to help you find someone who's local. Other states link to the IRS web site where you can also find local tax professionals by zip code.

FILING BY PHONE. Some states offer a separate TeleFile option. You call the state's toll-free number and input your state income tax information as prompted by the recorded message on the line. Almost all states require a TouchTone phone and limit this filing option to certain eligible taxpayers. However, one state—Colorado—lets you use either a TouchTone or rotary phone. And a couple of states let *any* full-time resident, regardless of the type or amount of income, use this filing method.

In some states, Telefile is a paperless filing method. You key in your personal identification number—sometimes the same self-select PIN used for the federal TeleFile, sometimes the PIN on the label to the TeleFile booklet, and sometimes an entirely unique code you can select. With paperless filing, you don't need to send a signature form or copies of W-2 forms to the state.

In other states, however, a separate signature form—a signature document in the TeleFile booklet or the state's version of Form 8453OL—must be completed. Some of these states merely require completion and retention of the form, but others require the form, along with copies of W-2 forms, to be mailed to the state after the return has been filed.

Fill-In Forms

Some states provide "fillable" forms that you can use to prepare your return. You input the information and the form does the calculations for you. But with this tax preparation option you can't:

- Save your information to return at a later time. You must finish whatever form you're working on or you'll lose the information.
- File the return electronically. You can print out a completed return to be signed and mailed in the usual way.

Getting Refunds

Like federal tax returns, using electronic filing methods ensure that you'll receive your returns quicker than if you filed a paper return. The promised refund time varies from state to state—but in all cases it's shorter than the time for refunds on paper returns.

As in the case of your federal return, you can opt to apply any state income tax refund from 2001 toward your state's estimated taxes in 2002. Once you select this option, you can't change your mind and recover the payment—until you file your 2002 return in 2003.

You may be able to receive your refund even quicker with a refund anticipation loan. You'll pay for the privilege, but if you need the cash very fast—a few days—this is the option to select. Refunds methods are explained in Chapter 3.

Paying Taxes Owed

In most states you can opt to pay your taxes by credit card—Discover, MasterCard or American Express. Or, you can opt to have your tax payment debited from your bank account. But check your state's payment options through the state web site or the instruction booklet you received. For example, some states only use one company through which you can charge your taxes—the IRS has two such approved companies.

Payment methods are explained in Chapter 3.

State-by-State Survey of Filing Options

The following brief descriptions of each state can alert you to your filing options (based on information for 2000 returns). All states are included below. Even though some do not have a state income tax, other information is provided.

You can only use a product that has been approved by your state ("authorized software"). Authorized software for preparing state income tax returns differs from state to state (states generally require commercial software companies to submit their products for approval, although one state awards authorization on a bidding basis). Some software can be used only to prepare returns while others can be used to both prepare and file returns electronically. Costs vary substantially—for example, some online software is free but there is

---

Do It Better . . .

If you live in a second (or third) state as a part-time resident, be sure to check filing requirements there. The same is true if you own property or conduct business in another state and must file a return there. Look for software that supports part-year and non-resident filing options.

a charge for *e-filing*. Some include one free state *e-filing* in the cost of *e-filing* the federal return.

Keep in mind that these options may change at any time—generally to be expanded for new opportunities. For example, states that require paper signature forms to be mailed after *e-filing* may eliminate this requirement in the future. Currently, the Quicken Tax Freedom Project, (QTFP) (www.quicken.com/freedom), with which you can prepare your federal and state return online and file it for free, is open only to those with adjusted gross income of $25,000 or less. In the state-by-state explanations that follow, the Quicken Tax Freedom Project is referred to as QTFP. Commercial products that were limited to simple returns last year may be available for more complex returns this year. So check you state's web site before you make your final decision on your filing options.

Where states do not provide their own directory of *e-file* providers—generally by zip code or area code—you can find one by zip code at the IRS web site (www.irs.ustreas.gov/prod/elec srs/efile-ind.html).

> **CAUTION**
>
> If you used TaxPrep last year to prepare and file your state return electronically, you're out of luck this year. This software is no longer in use. You'll have to select another authorized software this year.

ALABAMA. Paperless filing option is available.

ALASKA. While there is no state income tax, you must file to receive your Alaska Permanent Fund refund. You can do this directly through the state web site.

ARIZONA. *E-filing* is available, but can't be used if you're claiming a property tax credit or an alternative fuels credit. Authorized software for online and off-the-shelf use includes TaxACT, TaxCut, Complete Tax, Tax Brain, and TurboTax. You must complete Form 8454-OL, *Arizona Individual Declaration for Electronic Filing*, and mail it to the state within one day of receiving acknowledgment that the return has been accepted.

ARKANSAS. The state has its own TeleFile program (at www.ar-tax.org). The state return can also be prepared online and filed using TurboTax for the Web, TaxSlayer, TaxBrain.com, or CompleteTax. You can also prepare your return at Tax-engine.com, but you can't file it electronically—you'll have to print it out for mailing.

CALIFORNIA. You can prepare and file your return online for free if you are using CA Form 540 2EZ. You can use QTFP (www.quicken.com /freedom) or www.FileYourTaxes.com. To file your taxes online, you need a customer service number (CSN) that was sent to you in the mail. You can also obtain one online at the state site.

COLORADO. If you are a full-year resident you can use TeleFile—with a TouchTone or rotary phone. To file online you need to set up a new user ID (you can't use last year's number). You can do this at the state's *NetFile* web site.

CONNECTICUT. Free online preparation and filing is available through QTFP for eligible filers. You can use commercial sites to prepare your return online and file it: TaxSlayer, Turbo Tax for the Web, Complete Tax, H&R Block's Tax Cut, and TaxBrain.com. You can use the IRS self-select PIN for paperless filing or mail it to the Department of Revenue Services Form CT-8453-OL, *Income Tax Declaration for Electronic Filing by Individuals.*

DELAWARE. You can prepare and file your return for free at the state site—if you get a session ID number, you can return to complete your return at a later time. You can also prepare and file online using: Complete Tax, H&R Block, TaxBrain.com, Tax Slayer, and TurboTax for the Web.

DISTRICT OF COLUMBIA. You can Telefile using an 800 number. You can prepare and file your return online for free with QTFP if you are eligible. You can use these commercial sites to prepare your return online and file it: TurboTax for the Web and TaxSlayer.

FLORIDA. There is no income tax. But you can Telefile your intangibles tax if you owe less than $60.

GEORGIA. You can TeleFile your federal and state returns at the same time—one phone call to provide the information necessary to complete and file both returns. If you do, write your acknowledgment on Form 500-T and retain it with your tax records. You can prepare and file your return online for free with QTFP if you qualify. You can also use software to prepare the return and file it online using Complete Tax (online only), TurboTax, Tax Act, Tax Cut, and TaxSlayer. If you *e-file* your state return, you must complete GA-8453OL, *Georgia Individual Income Tax Declaration for Electronic Filing.* Do not mail in the form; retain it with your tax records.

HAWAII. You can use software to prepare your return and file it online. Use your Social Security number to register for online filing and then select your own password. You'll receive an e-mail confirmation that your return has been accepted or you can print the confirmation. Authorized software includes: Complete Tax (online only), Ultra Tax, Drake Tax Solutions, H&R Block, Taxwise, and Profiler.

IDAHO. You can use TeleFile if you received a TeleFile booklet. The process is paperless (no signature form or other forms need to be mailed to the state). You can *e-file* your state return with your federal return through the state web site. You can also prepare your return online and file it for free with QTFP. You can prepare your return online and file it through the commercial site, Complete Tax. You can find a local *e-file* provider by city at the state web site.

ILLINOIS. You can TeleFile if you received a TeleFile booklet. You can prepare and file online using 2nd Story, TurboTax for the Web, Tax & Accounting Software, H&R Block, Complete Tax, ezTaxReturn.com, and FileYourTaxes.com. You can use off-the-shelf software to prepare your return and then file it electronically using 2nd Story, Turbo Tax, Tax & Accounting Software, or H&R Block. You can locate a local *e-file* provider at the state onsite directory.

INDIANA. You can TeleFile your federal and state returns at the same time—one phone call to provide the information necessary to complete and file both returns. You can *I-file* with a number of different commercial companies.

IOWA. You can TeleFile using the PIN number or TeleFile information sent to you. You can prepare and file your return online for free (*web-file*) using the IA PIN on the mailing label of the short form booklet or TeleFile information sent to you. To web-file, you must complete your federal return first. You can use commercial software to prepare your return and then file it electronically. Authorized software includes: Complete Tax (online only), Tax Act, Tax Brain.com, TaxSlayer, and TurboTax. You can also use an *e-file* provider (use the IRS web site to find a local authorized provider). If you file electronically, you can use the IRS self-select PIN as your electronic signature. If you do not use the IRS self-select PIN, then you must sign and file Form IA 8453-OL.

KANSAS. All residents who filed in the prior year are eligible to TeleFile their returns (through October 15th) by downloading a worksheet (if your address has changed, then follow instructions). You can *PC-file* (you must use a PC format—Mac format is not recognized), but only if you have Broadband. Authorized software includes: Complete Tax (online only), H&R Block, TurboTax, TaxBrain.com, TaxSlayer, and Tax Engine. You can search for an authorized *e-file* provider by zip code.

KENTUCKY. You can TeleFile your federal and state returns at the same time—one phone call to provide the information necessary to complete and file both returns. You can prepare your return online and file it using the following commercial software: TaxACT and Turbo Tax for the Web.

LOUISIANA. You can prepare your return online and file it for free through the state's tax Web filing system. Eligible taxpayers can use also QTFP to prepare and file for free. You can also use commercial software. Authorized software includes: H&R Block, TurboTax, and TaxSlayer.

MAINE. You can TeleFile your return if you received a TeleFile booklet. You can prepare your return online and file it for free (I-file) at the state's web site, or if eligible, using QTFP. Or you can prepare your return online and file it using the following commercial software: Complete Tax and TurboTax for the Web. Authorized commercial software includes: H&R Block.

MARYLAND. You can prepare your return online and file it for free (I-file) at the state's web site, or if eligible, using QTFP. You can prepare your return online and file it electronically using commercial sites: FastRefund.net, TaxSlayer, Tax Cut, Complete Tax, Isonline.com, Tax & Accounting Software, TaxACT Online, and OrrTax Software. You can search for an authorized *e-file* provider at the state's web site.

MASSACHUSETTS. You can TeleFile your return if you are a full-year resident and meet certain criteria. Complete the TeleFile worksheet in the TeleFile booklet and then access the system with a Touch-Tone phone using your PIN or information from last year's return. You can prepare and file your return online for free at the state web site (Mac users okay) if you are a full-year resident and meet certain criteria. You can *e-file* using commercial software. Authorized software includes: Complete Tax (online only), Turbo-

Tax, Tax Cut, and HDVest. You can find a local *e-file* provider using the state web site.

MICHIGAN. If eligible, you can prepare your return online and file it free using QTFP. Or you can prepare your return online and file it electronically using commercial software: Complete Tax (online only), H&R Block, TurboTax, and TaxSlayer. If you *e-file*, you need Form MI-8453, *Michigan Individual Income Tax Declaration for Electronic Filing*. You can search for an authorized *e-file* provider at the state's web site.

MINNESOTA. You can prepare your return and file if free at Fidelity.com. Or you can prepare your return online and file it electronically using commercial software: TaxACT online or TurboTax for the Web.

MISSISSIPPI. You can TeleFile your return but you must sign and mail a *TeleFile* Signature Document to the state (the address you send it to depends on whether you're getting a refund or owe a tax). If eligible, you can prepare your return online and file it free using QTFP. Or you can prepare your return online and file it electronically using commercial software: Complete Tax (online only), TurboTax for the Web, and TaxSlayer. If you *e-file*, you need to mail in Form MS-8453, *Mississippi Individual Income Tax Declaration for Electronic Filing*.

MISSOURI. You can prepare your return and file it for free at the state's web site. Use the PIN number in the instruction booklet mailed to you. You can also use fill-in forms at the state's site—these will do calculations but cannot be filed electronically. You can print and sign them for mailing. To locate a local *e-file* provider, use the IRS web site.

MONTANA. If eligible, you can prepare your return online and file it free using QTFP. Or you can prepare your return online and file it electronically using commercial sites: TaxBrain.com or Complete Tax. You can search for an authorized *e-file* provider by zip code at the state's web site. There is no Telefile option.

NEBRASKA. You can TeleFile if you received a TeleFile booklet. You can also use fill-in forms ("fillable" forms) at the state's site—these will do calculations but cannot be saved or filed electronically. You can *e-file* using commercial software. Authorized software includes: Complete Tax (online only), TurboTax, and TaxSlayer. To *e-file* you need a 5-digit PIN on the label of your *e-file* booklet or call

800-742-7474 to obtain a PIN. You can jointly file your federal and state returns using an *e-file* provider.

NEVADA.　There is no state income tax but you can use the state site to find other state tax information such as the ad valorem property tax.

NEW HAMPSHIRE.　While there is no state income tax, there is a tax levied on interest and dividend income.

NEW JERSEY.　You can TeleFile using a TouchTone phone. Complete the worksheet in your TeleFile instruction booklet and use the NJ PIN on the booklet as your electronic signature. You can download free software to prepare your return from the state web site. To locate a local *e-file* provider, use the IRS web site.

NEW MEXICO.　You can use an online interactive program ("Pit-Net") at the state web site to prepare and file your return (through October 15th). Or if eligible, you can prepare your return online and file it free using QTFP. If payment is due, use a credit card or send a payment using Form PIT-PV. You can use commercial sites to prepare your return online and file it: Complete Tax, Tax-engine.com, and TaxBrain.com. You can buy commercial software to prepare your return and file it. Authorized software includes: Complete Tax, Tax Cut, Turbo Tax, and TaxSlayer. There is no TeleFile option.

NEW YORK.　You can use commercial sites to prepare your return online and file it: Complete Tax, TaxACT, TurboTax for the Web, Tax Cut, TaxSlayer. and TaxBrain.com. You must sign and mail Form IT-200-E, *Declaration for Electronic Filing of Income Tax Return*. To locate a local *e-file* provider, use the IRS web site.

NORTH CAROLINA.　If eligible you can prepare your return online and file it for free using QTFP. You can use commercial sites to prepare your return online and file it: Complete Tax, TaxACT, FileYourTaxes.com, Tax Cut, and Tax Slayer. You must sign and mail (along with any W-2s) Form NC-8453, *Affirmation for Electronic Filing*. You can find a local *e-file* provider at the state web site. There is no Telefile option.

NORTH DAKOTA.　You can use commercial sites to prepare your return online and file it: Complete Tax and TurboTax for the Web. There is no Telefile option.

OHIO.　You can use commercial sites to prepare your return online and file it: Complete Tax, HD Vest, Tax Cut, TaxSlayer, TurboTax for the Web, and TaxBrain.com. You can use commercial software to prepare your return and then file it electronically. Authorized software includes: Tax Act, Tax Cut, and TurboTax. There is no TeleFile option.

OKLAHOMA. You can TeleFile your federal and state returns at the same time—one phone call to provide the information necessary to complete and file both returns. You can use free software ("NetFile") at the state web site to prepare and file your state return along with your federal return. This option is open to all state residents. If you use the software, you must send in OTC Form 522EF as your signature form.

OREGON. If eligible, you can prepare your return online and file it for free using QTFP. No mail-in signature form is required. There is no separate commercial software and there is no TeleFile option.

PENNSYLVANIA. You can TeleFile if you received a TeleFile booklet or PA-40 booklet with a PIN. You can use commercial sites to prepare your return online and file it: Complete Tax, TurboTax for the Web, Tax Cut, Tax Act and TaxSlayer. You can buy commercial software to prepare your return and file it. Authorized software includes: Complete Tax, Tax Cut, TurboTax (and TurboTax for Mac), Tax Act, H&R Block, and TaxSlayer. You must complete and retain (don't mail) Form PA-8453, *Pennsylvania Individual Income Tax Declaration for Electronic Filing*. You can also use fill-in forms at the state web site to complete your return for printing, signing, and mailing.

RHODE ISLAND. You can use commercial sites to prepare your return online and file it: Complete Tax, Tax Cut, TurboTax for the Web, and H&R Block. There is no TeleFile option.

SOUTH CAROLINA. You can TeleFile if you received a TeleFile booklet. (this option is only for certain residents). You can use the state web site to prepare and file your return for free ("SCnetFile") This option is open to all state residents. You can use commercial sites to prepare your return online and file it: Complete Tax, TurboTax for the Web, Tax Cut, Tax Act and TaxSlayer. To locate a local *e-file* provider, use the IRS web site.

SOUTH DAKOTA. There is no state income tax but you can use the state web site to find unclaimed property (such as bank accounts) and other state tax information.

TENNESSEE. The state's income tax is limited to a tax on interest and dividend income. There is no *e-filing*.

TEXAS. There is no state income tax but you can use the state web site to learn about other state taxes, including property taxes.

UTAH. If eligible you can prepare your return online and file it for free using QTFP. You can use commercial sites to prepare your return online and file it: Complete Tax, TurboTax for the Web, and H&R Block. To locate a local *e-file* provider, use the IRS web site.

VERMONT. You can prepare and file your return for free at the state web site (*V-file*). There is no TeleFile option nor any authorized commercial software.

VIRGINIA. You can TeleFile if you received a TeleFile booklet and have a TouchTone phone. You can prepare and file your return for free at the state web site (*I-file*) or use an *e-file* provider.

WEST VIRGINIA. You can use commercial sites to prepare your return online and file it: Complete Tax, TurboTax for the Web, and TaxSlayer. Or you can use an *e-file* provider. There is no TeleFile option.

WISCONSIN. You can TeleFile but it is not a paperless process—you must sign and mail the signature document in the TeleFile booklet along with W-2 forms. If eligible, you can prepare and file your return for free using QTFP. Or you can use commercial sites to prepare your return online and file it: Complete Tax, TurboTax for the Web, and TaxACT. You can buy commercial software to prepare your return and file it. Authorized software includes: TaxAct, Tax Cut, Turbo Tax (and TurboTax for Mac), and TaxSlayer. You must mail in a signature form, Form 8453W-OL along with W-2 forms. To locate a local *e-file* provider, use the IRS web site.

WYOMING. There is no state income tax but you can check the web site for other state tax information.

CHAPTER 7

Preparing and Filing Other State Tax Forms

State online filing isn't limited to income tax returns. In the same way that you can *e-file* for an extension for federal taxes, you can *e-file* for an extension of time to file state income tax returns and to pay state estimated taxes.

But state taxes aren't limited to income tax. You may also have property taxes or other state taxes to contend with. You can use the Internet for these other state tax purposes to make tax compliance easier for you.

In this chapter you'll learn about:

- Filing extensions for state income tax returns.
- State estimated taxes.
- Property taxes.
- Other taxes.

Filing Extensions for State Income Tax Returns

If you are unable to file your state income tax return on time, you can obtain an automatic filing extension. As in the case of your federal return, this gives you more time to prepare your return but it doesn't extend the time for paying your state income taxes. This filing extension is available even if you cannot pay your taxes in full at this time.

Sometimes the filing extension is automatic—for example, you may have added time if you requested a federal filing extension. However, in other cases you need to take action to obtain the extension—if you fail to act before the tax deadline, you won't receive an extension and you'll be subject to late filing penalties.

Whether you obtain a state filing extension isn't dependent upon getting one for federal income tax purposes. For example, you can file your federal return on time but obtain a state filing extension.

There are several ways in which to get an automatic filing extension for state income tax returns:

- Request an automatic four-month filing extension for your federal return—this may also give you an automatic state extension. You request a federal extension by filing Form 4868, *Application for Automatic Extension of Time to File U.S. Individual Income Tax Return* (explained in Chapter 4).

- Request an extension by filing a state form—by mail or online. For example, Massachusetts grants extensions on its web site.

- Request an extension by telephone. You can also obtain a Massachusetts extension by telephone.

In some cases, obtaining an automatic four-month filing extension to file your federal income tax return acts as an extension for your state return—you don't need to take any action with your state to enjoy a state filing extension. But in other cases, you must make a separate request from your state. Table 7.1 details whether the federal extension gives you extra time to file your state return and, if not, what you must do to get a filing extension for your state income tax return.

Did You Know?

Your state filing deadline for state income tax returns may differ from the federal due date of April 15th. For example, Virginia's filing deadline is May 1st; Arkansas' and Louisiana's filing deadline are May 15th. Unsure of your state's deadline? Check the state web site (see Chapter 5).

TABLE 7.1 State Filing Extensions

STATE AND WEB SITE	IMPACT OF FEDERAL EXTENSION	ADDITIONAL INFORMATION
Alabama www.dor.state.al.us	Not valid for state purposes	File Form 4868A to obtain a 4-month extension (2 additional months in exceptional cases).
Arizona www.revenue.state.az.us/	Valid (if no tax is owed)	If tax is owed, use Form 204.
Arkansas www.state.ar.us/dfa	Valid	If no federal form is filed, use Form AR 1055.
California www.ftb.ca.gov	Valid (if no tax is owed)	6-month extension. If tax is owed, use Form 3519.
Colorado www.revenue.state.co.us	Valid	6-month extension if 90% of tax is paid by due date. Otherwise use Form DR 158-1.
Connecticut www.drs.state.ct.us	Not valid	Use Form CT-1040EXT for a 6-month extension.
Delaware www.state.de.us/revenue	Valid (if no tax is owed)	Use Form 1027 for an automatic $3\frac{1}{2}$ month extension (2 additional months in special circumstances by filing a copy of the federal extension Form 2688).
District of Columbia www.dccfo.com	Not valid	Use Form FR-127 for an automatic 4-month extension (2 additional months in special circumstances).
Georgia www2.state.ga.us/ departments/DOR	Valid	Automatic 6-month extension. If tax is owed, use Form IT-303.
Hawaii www.state.hi.us/tax/ tax.html	Valid (if tax is owed, then use federal Form 4868 but with state income and taxes)	If tax is owed, use Form N-101A for an automatic 4-month extension (Form N-101B for an additional 2 months in certain circumstances).

(Continued)

TABLE 7.1 *(Continued)*

STATE AND WEB SITE	IMPACT OF FEDERAL EXTENSION	ADDITIONAL INFORMATION
Idaho www.state.id.us.tax	Valid	Automatic 6-month extension. If tax is owed, use Form 51.
Illinois www.revenue.state.il.us	Valid (if no tax is owed)	If tax is owed, file Form IL-505-I.
Indiana www.in.gov/dor/	Valid (if at least 90% of tax has been paid)	2-month extension. If tax is owed, file Form IT-9.
Iowa www.state.ia.us/ government/drf	Valid (if no tax is owed)	6-month extension if 90% of tax is paid by April 30; if tax is owed, file Form IA 1040V with payment.
Kansas www.ink.org/public/kdor	Valid	If tax is owed, use Form K-40V to make payment (no separate extension form required).
Kentucky www.state.ky.us/	Valid	If tax is owed, use Form 40A 102.
Louisiana www.rev.state.la.us	Valid	For additional time (beyond the federal extension period) file Form R-6465.
Maine janus.state.me.us/revenue	There is an automatic 6-month extension (no form is required).	If tax is owed, use Form 4477ME as the extension payment voucher.
Maryland www.marylandtaxes.com	Valid (if no tax is owed)	If tax is owed, file Form 502E for a 4-month extension (2 additional months in certain circumstances).
Massachusetts www.state.ma.us/tax.htm	Valid (if no tax is owed)	If tax is owed, file Form M-4868 for a 6-month extension.
Michigan www.treas.state.mi.us	Valid	If tax is owed, use Form 4 or a copy of the federal extension to make a payment.
Minnesota www.taxes.state.mn.us	Valid (if no tax is owed)	6-month extension. If tax is owed, use Form M-13.

TABLE 7.1 *(Continued)*

STATE AND WEB SITE	IMPACT OF FEDERAL EXTENSION	ADDITIONAL INFORMATION
Mississippi www.mstc.state.ms.us	Valid (if no tax is owed)	If tax is owed, file Form 80-180 for a 4-month extension.
Missouri www.dor.state.mo.us	Valid (if no tax is owed)	If tax is owed, file Form MO-60 for a 4-month extension (2 additional months in certain circumstances).
Montana www.state.mt.us/revenue/	Valid	If tax is owed, use Form EXT-00 for making a payment.
Nebraska www.nol.org/hom/DNR	Valid (if no tax is owed)	If tax is owed, file Form 2688N.
New Hampshire www.state.nh.us	No form (or federal form) needed if tax is paid—7-month extension.	If tax is owed, use Form DP-59-A.
New Jersey www.state.nj.us/treasury/ taxation	Valid (if 80% of tax is paid)	If tax is owed, use Form JN-630 to obtain a 4-month extension (2 additional months in certain circumstances. Alternatively, file online without a payment.
New Mexico www.state.nm.us/tax	Valid	If no federal extension is filed, use Form RPD 41096.
New York www.tax.state.ny.us/	Valid (if no tax is owed) (send to state a copy of federal extension form marked at the top "NYS copy")	If tax is owed, use Form IT-370 for a 4-month extension (Form IT-372 for an additional 2 months in certain circumstances).
North Carolina www.dor.state.nc.us/	Valid	6-month extension. If no federal extension has been filed, use Form D-410.
North Dakota www.state.nd.us.taxdpt	Valid	If tax is owed, use Form F-101 to make payment.

(Continued)

TABLE 7.1 *(Continued)*

STATE AND WEB SITE	IMPACT OF FEDERAL EXTENSION	ADDITIONAL INFORMATION
Ohio www.state.oh.us/tax	Valid	If tax is owed, use Form IT-40P to make payment.
Oklahoma www.oktax.state.ok.us/	Valid (if no tax is owed)	If tax is owed, use Form 504.
Oregon www.dor.state.or.us	Valid	
Pennsylvania www.revenue.state.pa.us	Valid	If no federal extension has been filed, use Form REV-276.
Rhode Island www.dor.state.ri.us	Valid (if no tax is owed)	If tax is owed, use Form RI-4868 for 4-month extension (Form RI-2688 for 2 additional months in certain circumstances).
South Carolina www.dor.state.sc.us	Valid (if no tax is owed)	If tax is owed, use Form SC 4868.
Tennessee www.state.tn.us/revenue	Valid	6-month extension. If tax is owed, use Form INC 251.
Utah www.tax.ex.state.ut.us	Valid (if no tax is owed)	6-month extension. If tax is owed, file Form TC-546.
Vermont www.state.vt.us/tax	No	Use Form IN-151.
Virginia www.state.va.us/tax/tax/html	No	Use Form 760E for a 6-month extension from the May 1st due date.
West Virginia www.state.wv.us/taxrev/	Valid (if no tax is owed)	If tax is owed, use Schedule L for a 4-month extension.
Wisconsin www.dor.state.wi.us	Valid	If tax is owed, use Form I-ES to make a payment.

State Estimated Taxes

If your state income tax withholding on wages and other payments is insufficient to meet your state's estimated tax requirements, you may have to make estimated tax payments. Generally four payments are required for the year.

Like your federal return, you may be able to make state estimated tax payments online. For example, you may be able to charge your payments to your credit card—eliminating the need to file forms or payment vouchers with your state. Each state has its own requirements for estimated tax payments so you'll have to check your state tax site for its estimated tax payment options (see Chapter 5).

Property Taxes

If you own property, you are liable for property taxes—even if you don't live in the same state as your property. You can learn about when your local property taxes are due by checking with your state web site (see Chapter 5).

You may be able to pay your property taxes online. Some states already offer this option and other states are sure to follow suit.

Other Taxes

There are certain types of tax payments unique to certain states. If you live in Alaska, Florida, New Hampshire, or Tennessee, you'll want to see how online options can help you with these special taxes.

DIVIDEND PAYMENTS.   Residents of the oil-rich state of Alaska are in a unique position to *receive* tax rebates. Alaska residents may be entitled to a dividend through the Alaska Permanent Fund (APF)—in 2000 the dividend was almost $2,000 per state resident. You can apply for your dividend at the state's web site.

INTANGIBLES TAX.   Florida residents are subject to an intangibles tax on the value of stocks, bonds, mutual fund shares, and similar income items. The first $20,000 ($40,000 for joint filers) of such property is exempt. Property above the exemption amount is taxed at $1 per thousand dollars of

> **CAUTION**
>
> Watch the deadline for filing for claiming the APF dividend—it's not the usual April 15th tax deadline. There are no extensions available for this purpose. If you don't file for your dividend, you lose it.

Do It Better . . .

There's a discount for paying the intangibles tax early. The discount is 4% for payments in January and February, 3% in March, 2% in April, and 1% in May. The tax is late if paid after June 30.

Did You Know?

As yet, amended state income tax returns may *not* be filed online. If you find an error on your return—you omitted something or simply made a mistake—you must submit amended returns in paper form.

value. No tax is due if the amount is less than $600 *before* any discount. The tax can be paid using TeleFile if the amount of the intangibles tax is less than $60 (after the discount).

TAX ON INTEREST AND DIVIDENDS.   New Hampshire and Tennessee have a type of income tax that is largely levied against interest and dividends—wages, pensions and other earned income are exempt from the tax. For 2000 returns, there was no *e-filing* in New Hampshire and Tennessee, but this could change for 2001.

PART 3

Small Business Owner's Guide to Taxes Online

CHAPTER 8

Filing Business Income Tax Returns

Companies use computers every day in their operations. Computers help pay taxes and file returns for businesses. For many business owners this opportunity is both a great convenience and a big time-saver. And since time is money for business owners—using the computer for mandatory tasks is a cost cutter as well.

Both the IRS and various states have adopted new methods for business owners to meet their tax obligations through the Internet. Online filing of business income tax returns and online payment methods are two key ways for business owners to use the Internet to their advantage.

In this chapter you'll learn about:

- Benefits of *e-filing* business income tax returns.
- Selecting software for business income tax returns.
- Filing electronically.
- Paying taxes owed.

In the following chapter you'll learn about online reporting and payment options for employment taxes and other taxes—including estimated taxes for C corporations. And in Chapter 10 you'll see how the Internet can provide business owners with considerable tax assistance to help better manage the business and comply with tax obligations.

Benefits of *E-Filing* Business Income Tax Returns

E-filing isn't restricted to individuals—businesses can use this filing method as well. *E-filing* for business offers all of the same advantages over filing paper returns that it does for individuals:

- Convenience. Business owners don't keep nine to five hours and they don't necessarily work just five days a week. *E-filing* allows them to submit their returns when it's most convenient for them—after normal business hours or before the doors open in the morning.

- Ease. Business owners who use accounting software such as Peachtree or QuickBooks can tie their accounting data to their tax return to simplify tax return preparation. Tax preparation software can pick up this information from the accounting files. This integration feature is both quick and accurate.

- Accuracy. Returns prepared by software—online or with off-the-shelf products—generally have less than a 2% error rate. This compares with about a 21% error rate for manually prepared returns. When returns are filed electronically, the IRS checks that all information needed for processing the return is complete and accurate so that the return can be accepted as filed. This avoids questions about the return. And no business owner ever wants to invite closer scrutiny of the return.

- Proof of filing. When returns are accepted, an acknowledgment of acceptance is provided—generally within 48 hours after the return has been received. If there is a problem with the return—for example, necessary information has been omitted—the form is rejected. At that point, corrections can be made and the form can be resubmitted.

Working with Tax Professionals

Many business owners don't keep their own books and records or prepare their own tax returns—they let an accountant or other tax professional handle this aspect of the business. The professional may be in-house—a bookkeeper or comptroller—or on retainer—for example, an outside accountant.

Tax professionals today use more sophisticated software to prepare returns and can handle business returns of any complexity. If they are *e-file* providers they can also submit returns electronically provided that the forms and schedules are acceptable for *e-filing* (explained later in this chapter). So even if business owners don't prepare their own taxes, they can still be *e-filers*—through their tax professionals.

Whether business owners *should* work with professionals or handle tax obligations themselves is, of course, a question of ability, time, and cost. For small businesses—especially service-based companies—the chore of bookkeeping and tax compliance may be modest and easily handled by an owner with commercial software—assuming the owner has the knowledge of accounting and taxes sufficient to handle the work. Using professionals for bookkeeping and/or tax compliance may be just too costly an alternative.

For larger businesses—particularly inventory-based companies—the complexities of the tax rules may be better left to professionals. Tax professionals in this instance may handle not only tax compliance but also inventory management, cash flow matters, quarterly income statements, and other business matters. The cost of this professional assistance may be a necessary cost of doing business and is deductible.

Of course, businesses may keep their own books and records throughout the year, turning to professionals only to handle tax filings. This combination approach can help a business trim the cost of professional fees.

Finding tax professionals is discussed in Chapter 12.

Do It Better . . .

Fees for tax professionals can be deducted by the business. The timing of this deduction depends on the business' method of accounting. Cash method businesses deduct the payment when it's made. Accrual method businesses deduct the expense when all the events have occurred to fix the liability for payment—whether or not it has actually been made.

Selecting Software for Business Income Tax Returns

How is your company organized from a legal standpoint? Sole proprietorship, partnership, limited liability company (LLC), S corporation or C corporation? Your *type* of business organization dictates the income tax return that must be filed. This, in turn, affects both your software options and your online filing options. See Table 8.1 for a listing of which return you should file.

The type of business organization dictates the type of software needed to prepare and file a return.

- Sole proprietorships can use the software for individuals (see Chapter 2). Except for certain online sites that are limited to simple returns (such as Form 1040-EZ), most online sites and off-the-shelf software support Schedule C and Schedule C-EZ. The due date of the return for a sole proprietor is the due date for his or her individual income tax return—April 15th.

- Owners of pass-through entities (partners, LLC members, and S corporation shareholders) can also use the software for individuals to report their share of the business income. Owners of pass-through entities report their share of business income on Schedule E of Form 1040. Certain other pass-through items—such as an owner's share of first-year expensing or capital gains—are reported on other forms and schedules attached to Form 1040 as indicated on Schedule K-1s provided to owners by their pass-through entities.

- Partnerships and LLCs must use software that supports Form 1065. This form acts as an information return, reporting the

TABLE 8.1 Which Tax Return to File

TYPE OF BUSINESS ORGANIZATION	INCOME TAX RETURN TO BE FILED
Sole proprietorship	Schedule C or Schedule C-EZ attached to Form 1040
Partnership (including a general partnership and a limited partnership)	Form 1065
Limited liability company—LLC (including a limited liability partnership—LLP)	Form 1065 (unless the business opts to be taxed as a corporation)
S corporation	Form 1120S
C corporation	Form 1120

businesses' income and deductions and allocating items to owners. Partnerships and LLCs are *never* taxpayers at the federal level. The partnership return is due $3\frac{1}{2}$ months after the close of the business' tax year (for example, April 15th for a calendar year LLC).

- S corporations must use software that supports Form 1120S. This form primarily acts as an information return, reporting the corporations' income and deductions and allocating items to shareholders. S corporations generally are not taxpayers at the federal level, but there are limited exceptions. The S corporation return is due $2\frac{1}{2}$ months after the close of its tax year (for example, March 15th for a calendar year S corporation).

- C corporations must use software that supports Form 1120. C corporations are taxpayers subject to federal income tax. This form acts as a separate and unique income tax return for this type of entity. The corporate return is due $2\frac{1}{2}$ months after the close of the tax year—March 15th for calendar year C corporations.

TurboTax has products for preparing returns for all of these entities that are geared to the business owner who isn't a tax professional. TurboTax for Home & Business prepares Schedule C (or C-EZ) for sole proprietors. TurboTax Business prepares Forms 1065, 1120, and 1120S for other business entities. These products are integrated with accounting software such as QuickBooks and QuickBooks Pro. Business owners who wish to prepare their own tax returns for the business must use these products.

Or, business owners can turn to professionals who have a wide array of software products that enable the preparation of income tax returns for all types of business entities.

Do It Better . . .

Which software should a fiscal year C corporation use? Such a corporation—especially those with fiscal years ending in the first half of the year—may be required to file even though the IRS has not yet released new returns. If current forms and software are not yet available, use the prior year's versions with a notation at the top that they are for the current year. Since corporate tax brackets and other items aren't indexed for inflation (as they are for individuals), this should not affect tax liability.

Did You Know?

If you used PrepTax to prepare your 2000 business return—Form 1065, Form 1120, or Form 1120S, you'll have to find a new program for 2001 returns. This software is no longer being offered.

Electronic Filing of Business Income Tax Returns

Business owners can file their individual tax returns online as explained in Chapter 3. For example, individuals who use TurboTax Home & Business to prepare their Schedule C along with Form 1040 can file their returns online from an in-home or office computer. However, only certain other business returns can be filed electronically at this time—it is expected that eventually all returns will be able to be filed online.

The following is a list of forms and schedules that could be filed online for 2000 returns:

- Form 1065, *U.S. Partnership Return of Income.*
- Schedule D of Form 1065, *Capital Gains and Losses.*
- Schedule F of Form 1040, *Profit or Loss From Farming.*
- Schedule K-1 of Form 1065, *Partner's Share of Income, Credits, Deductions, Etc.*
- Form 3468, *Investment Credit.*
- Form 4562, *Depreciation and Amortization.*
- Form 4684, *Casualties and Thefts.*
- Form 4797, *Sale of Business Property.*
- Form 4835, *Farm Rental Income and Expense.*
- Form 5884, *Work Opportunity Credit.*
- Form 6198, *At-Risk Limitations.*
- Form 6252, *Installment Sale Income.*
- Form 6478, *Credit for Alcohol Used as Fuel.*
- Form 6765, *Credit for Increasing Research Activities.*
- Form 8275, *Disclosure Statement.*
- Form 8275-R, *Regulation Disclosure Statement.*
- Form 8283, *Noncash Charitable Contributions.*

- Form 8309, *Report of a Sale or Exchange of Certain Partnership Interests.*
- Form 8586, *Low-Income Housing Credit.*
- Form 8824, *Like-Kind Exchange.*
- Form 8825, *Real Estate Income and Expenses of a Partnership or an S Corporation.*
- Form 8826, *Disabled Access Credit.*
- Form 8830, *Enhanced Oil Recovery Credit.*
- Form 8835, *Renewable Electricity Production Credit.*
- Form 8845, *Indian Employment Credit.*
- Form 8846, *Credit for Employer Social Security and Medicare Taxes Paid on Certain Employee Tips.*
- Form 8861, *Welfare-to-Work Credit.*
- Form 8866, *Interest Computation under the Look-Back Method for Property Depreciated Under the Income Forecast Method.*

State Business Income Tax Returns

Businesses must file income tax returns in each state in which they "do business." What constitutes doing business isn't always clear. Businesses must have a "nexus"—meaning a connection—to a state in order to be subject to state income tax there. Generally this means having a physical presence in a state—maintaining an office or having a sales force or technicians in the state.

For sole proprietors and owners in pass-through entities (partnerships, LLCs, and S corporations), the owners must file returns in each

> **CAUTION**
>
> You don't need a sales force, made up of your employees, operating in another state from your main location, to create a nexus with another state for tax purposes. Independent sales representatives or technicians can create a nexus if they are essential to your business.

> **Example**
>
> Your headquarters are in Chicago but you have a sales staff operating from satellite offices in 10 other states. You are considered to be doing business in each of these states.

> **Example**
>
> You run an online sales business from Chicago. You ship to customers in every state. You're only doing business in Illinois—the state in which you have a physical presence—even though you have customers in every state.

CAUTION

The tax treatment of an entity may differ for federal and state tax purposes. For example, S corporations may be required to file and/or pay state income tax in some states, even though they are pass-through entities on the federal level. Different treatment may also apply to LLCs. Also, there may be different filing deadlines so be sure to check with each state in which the company does business.

state in which the entity does business and pay tax on their share of the business income.

For C corporations, which are separate taxpayers, the amount of tax paid to each state depends upon an apportionment of the taxable income of the business. This apportionment is necessary to prevent the business from paying tax twice on the same income. Generally an apportionment formula is made up of three factors (application of the formula is rather complicated):

- Payroll factor.
- Property factor.
- Sales factor.

Sole proprietors can use state online sites or off-the-shelf software to file their state income tax returns—most states merely require an attachment of the federal Schedule C or Schedule C-EZ. Similarly, owners of pass-through entities generally attach the federal Schedule E to their state income tax returns. For state income tax return preparation, see Chapter 5.

For other entities, do-it-yourself software is limited. This is one instance where you may need to rely on a tax professional—at least until such software for non-professionals becomes available.

> **Example**
>
> In 2001, an LLC did business in 19 states. The members of this LLC must file income tax returns in each of these states (assuming each state has an income tax) and pay state income tax on their share of the business income.

Filing Electronically

While *e-filing* for almost all taxpayers is the goal of Congress, at present electronic filing of business income tax returns is limited. If you are a sole proprietor filing Schedule C or Schedule C-EZ, then you can file your Form 1040 (plus business return) online. See Chapter 3.

> **CAUTION**
>
> Some state tax rules may differ from the federal rules. For example, a state may have different depreciation rules. This may require adjustments on a state income tax return.

If you are an owner in a pass-through entity—partner, member in an LLC, or S corporation shareholder—you can report your share of business income on your Form 1040. Your share of business income is reported on Schedule E of Form 1040 (other pass-through items are reported on other forms and schedules attached to Form 1040). Thus, you too can file your return online. See Chapter 3.

Partnership returns, Form 1065, used by both partnerships and limited liability companies, can be filed online, but only through an *e-file* provider. Large partnerships (those with 100 or more partners) *must* file electronically—other partnerships can choose to do so. A number of software companies have products that *e-file* providers can use to process partnership returns. For the 2000 return you could not use online or off-the-shelf software to file this type of return online.

> **CAUTION**
>
> In 2000, *e-filing* was barred to partnerships using fiscal year or short year. Check to see whether *e-filing* has been expanded for 2001 returns.

Corporate returns—Form 1120 for C corporations and Form 1120S for S corporations—may not as yet be filed online. This is so even through an *e-file* provider. However, this may change as the IRS moves to expand its *e-file* program.

Getting Refunds

Since partnerships don't pay income taxes, they aren't concerned with refunds. But C corporations (and in some cases S corporations) do pay taxes and may be owed returns. A corporation that overpays its income taxes may be entitled to a refund. Like individuals, there are several ways to obtain the refund:

- Have the refund—all or part—credited to estimated taxes for 2002.

- Have the government mail a check for the refund amount.
- Have the refund deposited directly into the corporation's bank account.

CREDIT TO ESTIMATED TAXES. The corporation can apply all or part of its refund of 2001 taxes to 2002 estimated taxes by merely indicating the dollar amount on the appropriate line on the corporate income tax.

REFUND BY MAIL. If the corporation does *not* take any affirmative action—applying the overpayment to next year's estimated taxes or requesting a direct deposit—a refund check will be mailed automatically for the amount of the overpayment shown on the return. It can take several weeks or more to receive a refund by mail.

DIRECT DEPOSIT. To use the direct deposit option for a prompter refund—typically within two weeks—the corporation must complete Form 8050, *Direct Deposit of Corporate Tax Refund*, and attach it to the income tax return for which the refund applies. This form simply includes the routing number, account number, and type of account—checking or savings—for the corporation's bank account. Unlike individual tax returns that provide space for including this information, corporations must furnish the information separately on this special form.

Paying Taxes Owed

Businesses have less flexibility in how they pay their taxes than individuals. While individuals can pay by check, credit card, or direct

---

Do It Better . . .

Instead of waiting to file a return to recover overpayments of estimated taxes, a corporation can obtain a quick refund by filing Form 4466, *Corporation Application for Quick Refund of Overpayment of Estimated Tax*. The overpayment must be at least 10% of the expected tax liability and at least $500. The form must be filed within two and one-half months of the close of the corporation's tax year—before it files a corporate income tax return. But the form can't be filed *before* the end of the tax year.

debit to a bank account, business payment options are more limited. The *size* of the business—not the *type* of business entity determines the available payment options.

ELECTRONIC TAX DEPOSITS. Large businesses (those that had aggregate federal tax deposits for corporate income tax, employment taxes, and excise taxes in excess of $200,000 two years ago) must pay their taxes via electronic transfer under the Electronic Federal Tax Payment System (EFTPS)—a tax payment and reporting system of the U.S. Treasury. Businesses that are required to use EFTPS but fail to do so may be subject to a 10% penalty.

If you are not *required* to pay your taxes by electronic transfer (your aggregate federal tax deposits didn't exceed $200,000 two years ago), you are still *permitted* to do so. Many small business owners find paying by electronic transfer to be convenient and easy. Here are some of the advantages of depositing your taxes electronically:

- You don't need any special equipment.
- There is no IRS fee for using EFTPS.
- You initiate payment—with your computer or a telephone call to your bank—24 hours a day, 7 days a week.
- You receive an acknowledgment number as your proof of payment.
- Security. Payment is made under your PIN number if you make a direct payment (or with security provided by your financial

Do It Better . . .

Learn about EFTPS by downloading IRS Publication 966, EFTPS, from the IRS web site at www.irs.gov.

Example

If your tax deposits first crossed the $200,000 threshold in 2001, you are not required to use EFTPS before 2003. If your tax deposits in 2000 first exceeded $200,000, you must start to use EFTPS in 2002 if you have not already done so.

institution). Either way, the IRS does not gain access to your bank account information.

EFTPS isn't merely for the payment of income taxes—something generally limited to C corporations. EFTPS can be used to pay a variety of taxes that any type of business may face, including:

- Corporate income taxes (Form 1120).
- Federal excise taxes—due quarterly (Form 720).
- FICA tax and income tax withholding on wages—due quarterly (Form 941).
- FUTA tax (Form 940).
- Employment taxes for agricultural workers (Form 943).

The payment of employment taxes and excise taxes is discussed in Chapter 9.

BANK DEPOSITS OF TAXES. If you don't use EFTPS you must deposit your taxes at an authorized depository (a bank that can accept these federal tax payment deposits) unless you are permitted to pay your tax with the return (discussed below). In this case, you use Form 8109, *Federal Tax Deposit Coupon*, to accompany your payment.

PAYMENT WITH THE TAX RETURN. In limited circumstances, you are not required to deposit your taxes—electronically or with a federal tax deposit coupon. Instead you can pay your taxes by check at the time you file your return. This payment option generally is limited to minimal amounts—for example, employment taxes can be paid by check with the quarterly return if the accumulated liability is less than $2,500.

Using EFTPS

To pay your taxes via an electronic transfer, you must enroll in EFTPS—the Electronic Federal Tax Payment System. To enroll in EFTPS—whether required to do so or voluntarily—call 1-800-945-

---

Did You Know?

About 2 million businesses, many of them small businesses, have already enrolled in EFTPS. Some of these businesses have done so voluntarily.

8400 or 1-800-555-4477 for your enrollment package, Form 9779, *Business Enrollment Form*. Complete the form you receive from the IRS and mail it to the EFTPS Enrollment Center (the address is in the package).

Indicate your payment method—direct payment or through a financial institution—by checking the appropriate box on your enrollment form. These payment methods are explained below.

After submitting your enrollment form, you'll then receive a Confirmation Package and Personal Identification Number (PIN). With this information in hand, you are now able to pay your taxes via electronic transfer.

As mentioned above you have two payment options under EFTPS:

- Direct payment to EFTPS. Using this method you initiate payment with your computer or telephone (a toll-free number). This is called the ACH Debit Method (check this box on your enrollment form).

- Through a financial institution. You initiate payment using a payment service from your bank or other financial institution. Some offer a same-day payment option. This is called the ACH Credit Method (check this box on your enrollment form). If you opt for this payment method, then the EFTPS PIN is only for inquiry purposes—it won't be used by you to initiate your payment. You'll receive separate instructions from your financial institution on how to authorize a payment—perhaps another PIN to use in its payment process.

MAKING A PAYMENT. If you're using the direct payment method, then at least one business day prior to the tax due date (before 8:00 P.M. ET), you access EFTPS by computer or telephone. The system then prompts you for certain information to make your payment. Once

---

Do It Better . . .

Before enrolling in the ACH Credit Method, make sure your financial institution offers ACH Credit origination services. Also check with the costs, deadlines, and other details of using its services to pay your taxes to see if this is the payment method you'd prefer to use.

the payment is processed, you receive an acknowledgment number—retain it as your proof of payment. The payment is debited against your designated account. The transaction is then posted to your account on the tax due date.

If you're making a payment through a financial institution, then one or two days before the tax is due you should initiate payment with your financial institution. Follow its guidelines on *when* you must initiate payment and *how* to do it. For example, ask about its ACH processing deadline so you won't miss it. After you follow bank procedures, the payment is debited from your account and transferred to the U.S. Treasury's account. Your bank may offer same-day payment—for a higher fee.

> **CAUTION**
>
> Direct payment by means of computer can only be done if you have a Window-based system. Mac users who want to use the direct payment method must telephone their financial institution.

WAREHOUSING YOUR PAYMENT. You can schedule a payment to be made up to 30 days in advance. This allows you to make your payments even if you're unavailable at the tax payment due date—for example, you're going to be out of town on business at the payment due date.

Do It Better . . .

Having any problems or questions about EFTPS? There's a Customer Service Center that's open Monday through Friday, 8:30 A.M. to 8 P.M. ET. Call 1-800-945-8400 or 1-800-555-4477.

Alert

At the time this book went to press, the IRS had just announced a new payment option to allow individuals and businesses to pay online through EFTPS-OnLine. For details see www.eftps.gov.

CHAPTER 9

Filing Employment Taxes and Other Returns

Income taxes are only one aspect of business operations. There are several other tax obligations that business owners must comply with—and taking care of these obligations online can make things a little easier for them.

If a business has *any* employees, including shareholders of corporations who work for their companies, employment taxes must be paid and employment tax returns must be filed. If the business makes certain payments, for example, fees to independent contractors, then information returns must be filed to report these payments to the IRS. If the business collects sales taxes, it must pay over these amounts and file sales tax returns. Excise taxes may also be due. And if the business has a qualified retirement plan, it may have to file annual information returns with the Department of Labor.

But complying with these many obligations has become easier—and often less costly—due to the advent of online filing opportunities. Returns can be filed online and taxes can be paid by means of electronic transfers or, in some cases, by charges to credit cards.

In this chapter you'll learn about:

- Employment taxes.
- Information returns.
- Other taxes and returns.

Employment Taxes

Tax Obligations

If you have *any* employees, you automatically have employment tax obligations. If you work for your business, you are considered an employee only if you are a shareholder in the corporation—C or S. If you are a sole proprietor, partner, or member in an LLC, you are *not* an employee of your business, no matter how many hours your put in or how important your work is for the company. In this case, you are a self-employed person and therefore not subject to employer withholding.

Employment tax obligations include:

- Withholding of income tax on employee compensation. Some types of compensation are exempt from withholding. Withholding may apply not only for federal income tax purposes but state income tax purposes as well.
- Employer payment of Social Security tax of 6.2% on wages up to a wage base limit ($80,400 in 2001). This wage base adjusts annually for inflation.
- Withholding of the employee share of Social Security tax—6.2% on wages up to a wage base limit ($80,400 in 2001). This wage base adjusts annually for inflation.
- Employer payment of Medicare tax of 1.45% on all wages (there is no wage base limit).
- Withholding of the employee share of Medicare tax—1.45% on all wages (there is no wage base limit).
- Employer payment of federal unemployment tax (FUTA)—6.2% on the first $7,000 of wages paid to each employee during the year. However, the percentage may be reduced by up to 5.4% for state unemployment tax payments. If you can claim this maximum credit, then the FUTA tax rate drops to 0.8%.
- Employer payment of state unemployment insurance. The state dictates the percentage of wages paid as an unemployment tax based on the company's unemployment experience (with a min-

imum percentage assigned for the first year that the company is in business and has no unemployment experience).

Employers must also provide employees with Form W-2, *Wage and Tax Statement*, by January 31st of the year following the year in which the wages were earned. A copy of Form W-2 must be submitted to the Social Security Administration (SSA) no later than February 28th of the year following the year in which the wages were earned. Employers who *e-file* wage statements gain addition time to submit them to the SSA—April 1, 2002. *E-filing* for wage statements is discussed later in this chapter.

To learn more about your employment tax obligations, see IRS Publication 15, Circular E, *Employer's Tax Guide*, IRS Publication 15A, *Supplemental Employer's Tax Guide*, and IRS Publication 15B, *Employer's Guide to Fringe Benefits*, all of which are available at the IRS web site. These three guides form the employer's bible on employment tax obligations.

REPORTING TIPS ONLINE. Employees are required to report tips of $20 or more earned in the prior month, to their employers. Employees of restaurants and other businesses where tipping is customary can now report tips to their employers electronically. Employers can set up their own electronic reporting systems for this purpose.

There is no standard online tip-reporting statement that employees must use for this purpose. But the tip information statement filed online must contain the same information that would be reported on a paper statement, Form 4070, *Employee's Report of Tips to Employers*.

- Name, address, and Social Security number of the employee.
- Name and address of the employer.
- Period for which the statement is being furnished.
- The total amount of tips received during this period.

Did You Know?

Self-employed business owners don't really escape employment taxes. They are liable for both the employer and employee share of Social Security and Medicare taxes. They pay this obligation as self-employment tax along with their individual income taxes. However, self-employment income is not subject to unemployment tax—on the federal or state levels.

CAUTION

If you are an employer who uses an electronic reporting system for tip reporting by employees, keep good records. You must be able to furnish a hard copy of the electronic tip statement if the IRS requests it.

The electronic statement must be "signed" by the employee. This can be an electronic signature—any means that verifies and authenticates that it is the statement of a particular employee.

To help employees report their tips, employers can provide employees with Form 4070A, *Employee's Daily Record of Tips.* You may wish to create an online version of this form for your employees to use for tracking their tips on a daily basis.

To encourage employee reporting of tips, the IRS has developed certain programs to educate employees about reporting in order to avoid examinations. The Tip Rate Determination Agreement (TRDA) is for employers in the food and beverage industry and the gaming industry; Tip Reporting Alternative Commitment (TRAC) is only for employers in the food and beverage industry and the cosmetology and barber industry. These programs are expected to expand in the future to other industries in which tipping is customary.

In exchange for setting up the education program for your employees, the IRS agrees not to examine you on tip reporting for the term of the agreement. This means you won't be subject to underpayment of FICA taxes during the term of the agreement. You can find information about these programs and how to initiate them at www.irs.gov/bus_info/msu-info.html.

STATE EMPLOYMENT TAX OBLIGATIONS. You are required to withhold state income tax for the state in which employees work. You may *opt* to withhold income tax for the state in which employees live.

If you have a multistate operation and have employees who work in more than one state, you must withhold state income tax for *each* state in which they work. For withholding purposes, you must apportion

Example

Your business is located in New Jersey. Some of your employees are New York residents. You *must* withhold New Jersey income tax from their wages. You *may* withhold New York income taxes from their wages.

their wages to each state—for example, on the basis of the number of days worked in each location or on some other reasonable basis.

To learn about your federal and state employment tax reporting obligations at a single web site click on www.tax.gov.

Online Filing

Online filing isn't restricted to income taxes. Employers can file employment tax returns online in several ways:

- Your tax professional that uses IRS-approved software for processing.
- Commercial filing services.
- Payroll service providers approved for *e-filing*.

If you decide to *e-file* your employment tax returns, select the method best suited for your situation. Consider cost, convenience, and other factors. Filing your employment returns electronically does *not* extend the time for filing—you have the same due date as paper returns. You can only use electronic filing for current returns—*e-filing* cannot be used for late or amended returns.

YOUR TAX PROFESSIONAL. Your accountant may have the capability of *e-filing* your employment tax returns. Ask whether this option is open to you—and what you'll be charged for the service.

COMMERCIAL FILING SERVICES. You can use online web sites to file your employment forms for you—for a modest fee (generally under $4 per form). You don't have to purchase any software or pay any subscription fees. You merely input your tax information on a secured web site. You will find a listing of some of these sites in Table 9.1.

These sites can also complete W-2 forms using your financial data. Then they will print and mail a copy to employees as well as file them electronically with the Social Security Administration.

PAYROLL SERVICE PROVIDERS. The outside company that handles your payroll may be able to handle your payroll taxes as well. Table 9.2 lists the IRS approved payroll service providers.

Employers can file the following employment tax forms online:

- Form 940, *Employer's Annual Federal Unemployment (FUTA) Tax Return.*

TABLE 9.1 Commercial Tax Filing Services

COMPANY	SITES	COST
1-800FileTax	www.filetax.com	variable
C&S Technologies, Inc.	www.esmarttax.com	variable
FileTaxes.com	www.irsus.com/filetaxes.htm	$3.49 per form
National Tax Online Inc.	www.nationtax.com	$2.95 per transaction
U.S. Tax Center	www.center4debtmanagement.com/ BusinessTax.shtml	$2.95 per transaction

TABLE 9.2 Payroll Service Providers

COMPANY	TELEPHONE	SERVICES
Automatic Data Processing Inc. (ADP) www.adp.com	800-255-5237	*e-filing* of Forms 941, W-2 and 1099; payment to EFTPS
Federal Liaison Services (FLS) www.fls.com	972-239-8881	*e-filing* of Forms 941; payments to EFTPS

- Form 940EZ, *Employer's Annual Federal Unemployment (FUTA) Tax Return.*
- Form 941, *Employer's Quarterly Federal Tax Return.*

In addition some states also allow for online filing of state employment tax returns. These may relate to state income tax withholding and state unemployment insurance. For more information about online filing for state employment tax forms, see STAWRS.

Did You Know?

The IRS hopes that 6 million businesses will be filing their employment tax returns online by 2003. More than 2.5 million already participate in online filing and enrollment of new businesses is proceeding at the rate of about 6,500 each week.

E-FILING WITH THE SOCIAL SECURITY ADMINISTRATION (SSA). Whether you have one or 1,000 or more employees, you can submit copies of W-2 forms as well as Form W-3, *Transmittal of Income and Tax Statements*, electronically to SSA using its Online Wage Reporting Service (OWRS). You must register with SSA and receive both a PIN and password needed for online access. You receive the PIN immediately and the password in 10 to 14 days. For registration and more information about the SSA online filing program see www.ssa.gov/employer/esohome.htm.

> **CAUTION**
>
> If you file 250 or more of any type of information return, you *must* use magnetic media or electronic filing—you can't use paper returns.

MAKING PAYMENTS. You can pay your taxes—income tax withholding, withholding of the employee share of FICA, the employer share of FICA, and FUTA tax—by check, direct debit to your bank account, or by using the Electronic Federal Tax Payment System (EFTPS). Payment via EFTPS—enrollment and the payment process—is explained in greater detail Chapter 8.

If you use a payroll service, you can also make payment through the payroll company—if they enroll in EFTPS.

Do It Better . . .

If you registered with the Social Security Administration to file W-2's electronically, you can submit forms for wages paid in 2001 from January 7, 2002, through Apirl 1, 2002.

Do It Better . . .

Before authorizing your payroll company to make employment tax payments on your behalf, ask about the fees, deadlines, and other pertinent information. Make *very* clear which taxes they should pay on your behalf. Even if you opt to pay through your payroll company, you should also enroll in EFTPS so you'll always have the flexibility of paying directing if you have a problem with the payroll company.

LATE OR UNDERPAYMENT PENALTIES.   If you don't pay enough employment taxes, you may be subject to penalties on the underpayments. The amount of the penalty depends on the size of the underpayment and how late you are in making the payment. If amounts are not timely deposited or properly deposited, penalty rates apply (see Table 9.3).

You can use an online site to compute your penalty—and possibly minimize the amount of the penalty. TimeValue Software provides a penalty computation service online at www.taxpenalty.com.

Filing by Telephone

Some businesses may be able to file their quarterly Form 941 by telephone instead of submitting it by mail or electronically. Under the IRS 941TeleFile system, businesses that receive 941TeleFile instructions and a Tax Record booklet and meet the qualifications of a "small business" detailed below can use a TouchTone phone to meet this filing obligation.

You are eligible to use the 941TeleFile option if you meet *all* of the following requirements (in addition to receiving the booklet). You:

- Are a monthly depositor for the entire quarter.
- Have been in business for the previous 12 months.
- Have not changed your business name or employer identification number (EIN) during the previous quarter.
- Do not have seasonal employees.

TABLE 9.3 Deposit Penalties

PENALTY	TARDINESS
2%	Deposits made 1 to 5 days late
5%	Deposits made 6 to 15 days late
10%	Deposits made 16 or more days late (and amounts paid within 10 days of the date of the first notice the IRS sent asking for the tax due)
10%	Deposits made at an unauthorized financial institution, paid directly to the IRS, or paid with the tax return (unless permitted to do so)
10%	Amounts subject to electronic deposit requirements but not deposited using EFPTS
15%	Amounts still unpaid more than 10 days after the date of the first notice the IRS sent asking for the tax due, or the date after which you receive notice and demand for immediate payment, whichever is earlier.

- Are not required to complete any schedules or attachments.
- Only have fractions of cents adjustments.
- Want to claim Advance Earned Income Credit payments made to low-income workers.

The 941TeleFile option in an interactive program that prompts you to key into the telephone keypad the required information. The system repeats your entries to verify accuracy and lets you make corrections, if needed, before you proceed. At the end of the call, the system immediately figures your tax liability and any overpayment or balance due. You can then simultaneously choose to pay any balance due using the direct debit method (see Chapter 3).

To use this method merely key in your bank account information (the type of account—checking or savings, the account number and the routing number) when prompted to do so. If payment is returned by the financial institution—for example, for insufficient funds or incorrect information—the IRS will notify you by letter and instruct you where to send a check. But you're responsible for any penalties and interest that result (unless the Treasury is responsible for causing an incorrect amount of funds to be withdrawn).

Finally, the 941TeleFile system prompts you to key in your Social Security number and the first five letters of the individual authorized to file (an officer, member, or agent of the taxpayer) or the entire name if less than five letters. This acts as your electronic signature for the telefiled return. You'll then receive a confirmation number as your proof of filing.

Some states—for example, in Florida if there are 15 or fewer employees—have TeleFile for employment tax returns. Check with your state's web site for its employment tax filing options.

Do It Better . . .

To inquire about payments made through a direct debit to your account, call the Treasury Financial Agent at 888-353-4537. But wait at least five days after the return is filed to make your inquiry. If you believe there's an error in the amount withdrawn from the account, call the IRS immediately at 800-829-1040.

Did You Know?

Paying employment taxes through a direct debit to your bank account is free (in contrast to credit card payments for personal income taxes that are subject to a 2.5% convenience fee). The payment is displayed on your monthly bank statement as a *United States Treasury Tax Payment*.

STAWRS

The IRS, the Department of Labor (DOL), the Small Business Administration (SBA), the Social Security Administration (SSA), the Office of Management and Budget (OMB), and several states and private organizations are working together to make employment tax filing easier and less burdensome on small businesses in several ways:

- A one-step process ("single point filing") for Forms W-2. This means that filing with the IRS will automatically satisfy state law requirements. The IRS forwards the information to the applicable state.

- A one-step process for filing quarterly employment tax returns. An electronic filing pilot project was completed in Iowa in 2000 and a paperless filing program was completed in Montana in 2000. This one-step process is now expected to expand to other states.

- Simplified requirements project to create an electronic transmission method for Form 8850, *Pre-Screening for Work Opportunity and Welfare-to-Work Credits*. This will ensure that eligible employees qualify for these credits if their expiration dates are extended beyond December 31, 2001.

- Customer Service projects to enable employers to access employment tax, wage, and industry information online. One project will enable the IRS to issue employer identification numbers (EINs) online. Form SS-4, *Application for an Employer Identification Number*, will no longer require a manual signature.

- Harmonized federal and state tax and wage codes. This would, for example, establish a single definition of "wages" for all tax purposes at both the federal and state levels. More specifically, a Harmonized Wage Code would be created for income tax withholding purposes (HWC/ITW) and another code would be created for unemployment insurance (HWC/UI).

Did You Know?

Some of the goals of STAWRS are already in the pilot program stage. Check with your state on whether you can use any of the STAWRS' features.

These aims are being addressed through the *Simplified Tax and Wage Reporting System (STAWRS)*. For information about STAWRS, click on:

- Employers.gov at www.employers.gov/stawrs/index.htm.
- Biz.gov at www.tax.gov/1stop.htm.

Information Returns

Reporting Obligations

If the business makes certain payments, special information returns are required. These returns are given to the payment recipients and also sent to the IRS to alert the government to the payments. The IRS uses information returns to cross-check tax reporting. For example, if a business makes a payment to an independent contractor and the amount is reported on an information return, IRS computers can check that the independent contractor has reported the same amount as income.

The following is a brief rundown of reporting requirements for information returns for payments made:

- Form 1099-A, *Acquisition or Abandonment of Property*. Information about the acquisition or abandonment of property in any amount.
- Form 1099-B, *Proceeds from Broker and Barter Exchange Transactions*. Barter exchange transactions and sales or redemptions of securities, futures transactions, and commodities in any amount.
- Form 1099-C, *Cancellation of Debt*. This form is issued only by a business with a significant trade in lending money. The form is issued if the cancellation is $600 or more.
- Form 1099-DIV, *Dividends and Distributions*. Dividends paid on stock, distributions from mutual funds, and liquidation distributions. For small businesses, this form must be issued on stock distributions of $10 or more and liquidations of $600 or more.

- Form 1099-INT, *Interest Income*. This form must be issued by payers of interest of $10 or more.

- Form 1099-MISC, *Miscellaneous Income*. This form covers a variety of payments: royalties of $10 or more, rents, prizes and awards of $600 or more, payments to crew members by fishing boat owners or operators in any amount, payments to non-employees (e.g., independent contractors, subcontractors, and corporate directors) of $600 or more, gross proceeds payable to attorneys of any amount, crop insurance proceeds of $600 or more, and fish purchases paid in cash for resale of $600 or more.

- Form 1099-OID, *Original Issue Discount*. This form applies only to original issue discount, a type of interest payment, of $10 or more.

- Form 1099-R, *Distributions from Pensions, Annuities, Retirement or Profit-Sharing Plans, IRAs, Insurance Contracts, Etc.* Company retirement plans must issue this information return for payments of $10 or more.

- Form 1099-S, *Proceeds from Real Estate Transactions*.

This list of forms is not all inclusive. There are other information returns for distributions from qualified state tuition programs, long-term care and accelerated death benefits, medical savings accounts, cooperatives, gambling winnings, currency transactions, and more. For an explanation of information returns filing requirements see *General Instructions for Forms 1099, 1098, 5498, and W-2G*, at www.irs.gov.

Generally information returns apply only to payments made to individuals and not to corporations or partnerships. However, you must report payments to corporations in the following circumstances:

- Medical and health care payments (Form 1099-MISC).

- Withheld federal income tax or foreign tax.

- Barter or exchange transactions (Form 1099-B).

- Substitute payments in lieu of dividends and tax-exempt interest (Form 1099-MISC).

- Interest or original issue discount paid or accrued to a regular interest holder of an REMIC (Form 1099-INT or Form 1099-OID).

- Acquisitions or abandonments of secured property (Form 1099-A).

- Cancellation of debt (Form 1099-C).
- Payments of attorneys' fees and gross proceeds paid to attorneys (Form 1099-MISC).
- Federal executive agency payments for services (Form 1099-MISC).
- Fish purchases for cash (Form 1099-MISC).

You must report payments to partnerships of $600 or more made in the course of your business. For example, if you paid an architectural firm operating as a partnership $1,000, you must report the payment on Form 1099-MISC.

Information returns aren't only for payments you make. You may also be required to file information returns to report payments you receive. These payments include:

- Form 1098, *Mortgage Interest Statement*. For mortgage interest (including points) of $600 or more received in the course of business (i.e., homesellers holding purchase money mortgages are not subject to reporting requirements).
- Form 1098-E, *Student Loan Interest Statement*. For student loan interest of $600 or more received in the course of business.
- Form 1098-T, *Tuition Payment Statement*. For tuition, related expenses, and scholarships.
- Form 8300, *Report of Cash Payments Over $10,000 Received in a Trade or Business*. If you received such a payment in one transaction (or two or more related transactions) in the course of your business, you must report the transaction to the payer and the IRS.

FILING DEADLINE. In most cases, you must provide the payment recipient ("payee") with an information return no later than January 31st of the year following the year of payment regardless of the tax year of your business. Thus, even if you have a June 30th fiscal year, you are still obligated to provide the payee with an information return by January 31st for a payment made in the preceding calendar year.

You must file the information return with the IRS by February 28th (or, in the case of cash transactions over $10,000, within 15 days of the transaction). However, if you opt to file electronically you have an additional one-month filing deadline—to March 31st. Since March 31, 2002, is a Sunday, the electronic filing deadline is April 1, 2002.

You may request an extension of time to file information returns by submitting Form 8809, *Request for Extension of Time to File Information Returns* no later than the filing deadline. If your request is granted, you have an additional 30 days to file.

PENALTIES. If you fail to file the required returns on time or include incorrect information, you may be subject to a penalty. The amount of the penalty depends on *when* you file correct information:

- $15 per information return if you correctly file within 30 days. The maximum penalty is $75,000 per year ($25,000 for small businesses, explained below).

- $30 per information return if you correctly file more than 30 days after the due date, but by August 1st. The maximum penalty in this case is $150,000 per year ($50,000 for small businesses).

- $50 per information return if you file after August 1st or you do not file required information returns. The maximum penalty is $250,000 per year ($100,000 for small businesses).

- $100 per information return if the failure to file or incorrect information is due to intentional disregard of the filing or correct information requirements. There is no maximum penalty.

"Small businesses" are those with average annual gross receipts for the three prior years (or the period of existence if shorter) of $5 million or less.

Example

You file a paper return on February 28th. You have until March 30th to file a correct information return in order to avoid penalty.

Preparing Information Returns

Information returns can be a particularly time-consuming chore—depending on the number of returns you have to complete. There are several ways to prepare information returns:

- Your tax professional that uses IRS-approved software for processing.

- Commercial filing services—from data provided by use. These companies both prepare your information returns and then file them online. For the cost of this method, see online filing of employment tax returns.

- TurboTax Home & Business or TurboTax Business. If you use these products to prepare your business income tax returns, you can also use them to prepare 1099s. This can be particularly helpful if you use independent contractors in your business.

Online Filing

Online filing of information returns offers several key and even unique advantages over paper returns:

- Forms are processed quickly and errors are virtually eliminated.

- Added time is available for online filing of information with the IRS. Whereas the regular due date for information returns is February 28th, online filers have an additional month—to March 31st.

The IRS has created a special online filing system for information returns called Filing Information Returns Electronically (FIRE). Information returns currently within the FIRE program include:

- Form 1099-A, *Acquisition or Abandonment of Security Property*.

- Form 1099-DIV, *Dividends and Distributions*.

- Form 1099-INT, *Interest Income*.

- Form 1099-MISC, *Miscellaneous Income*.

- Form 1099-S, *Proceeds from Real Estate Transactions*.

CAUTION

While *e-filing* gives more time to file information returns with the IRS, it doesn't change the due date for furnishing these forms to payees, such as independent contractors.

You can file the returns yourself, with a computer and Internet connection. Or you can use an IRS-approved business *e-file*

Do It Better . . .

For details about the FIRE program, and updates as they occur, click on www.irs.gov/elec_svs/fire-sys.html. You can also call for information at 304-263-8700 (not a toll-free number).

---

provider. To see a listing of IRS-approved business *e-file* providers, click on www.irs.gov/elect_svs/abp.html.

There are also commercial online sites (see the above site under Employment Taxes) that can file 1099s for under $4 per form. The price includes both submission to the IRS or other government agency as well as printing and mailing the form to the recipient or employee.

Other Taxes and Returns

Corporate Estimated Taxes

Like individuals, C corporations (and S corporations in limited circumstances), which are separate taxpaying entities, must pay quarterly estimated taxes if tax liability for the year is $500 or more. The failure to pay sufficient estimated taxes can result in penalties on the corporation.

Estimated taxes are figured on Form 1120-W, *Corporation Estimated Tax*. But this form isn't filed with the IRS—it's merely a worksheet for the business. The corporation is subject to different payment requirements than individuals and has several ways to min-

---

Do It Better . . .

Corporations can obtain quick refunds of overpaid estimated taxes—they don't have to wait to file their income tax returns for this purpose. For a quick refund—which can be used to generate working capital for the business—file Form 4466, *Corporation Application for Quick Refund of Overpayment of Estimated Tax*, after the close of the year but within the first 2½ months of the following year (remember corporate income tax returns for calendar year corporations are due March 15th).

imize or avoid penalties for underpayments. For information about corporate estimated taxes see IRS Publication 542, *Corporations*, that can be downloaded from the IRS web site. The information is also on the Small Business Resource Guide, a free CD-ROM that can be ordered online at the "Small Business Corner" at www.irs.gov.

Estimated taxes are paid in the same manner as corporate income taxes—generally through electronic transfer or with a federal tax deposit coupon to an authorized depository—no special form is filed for estimated taxes. These payment methods are discussed in Chapter 8.

Qualified Retirement Plans

Businesses that maintain qualified retirement plans—pension, profit-sharing, money purchase, 401(k), or other plans—generally are required to file an information return in the Form 5500 series. (No information returns are required for Simplified Employee Pensions or SEPs, and SIMPLE-IRAs.) These information forms generally are prepared by plan administrators, which in small businesses, may be the business owner. No tax is due with these forms—they're merely for informational purposes.

TAX OBLIGATIONS. Forms in the 5500 series are due by the last day of the seventh month following the end of the plan year. For example, a calendar year profit-sharing plan must file this information return no later than July 31st.

Even though the form is an IRS form, it isn't filed with the IRS. The form is filed with the Department of Labor's Pension and Welfare Benefits Agency in Lawrence, Kansas. If you fail to file the return on time, you may be subject to a penalty of $25 per day (up to $15,000).

If you cannot meet this filing deadline, you can request a filing extension by filing Form 5558, *Application for Extension of Time to File Certain Employee Plan Returns*. The request must be made no

---

Did You Know?

Tax returns generally are confidential. If the IRS discloses confidential information other than permitted by law, it can be subject to severe penalties. But forms in the 5500 series aren't confidential. They're open to public inspection—by plan participants or anyone else.

later than the filing deadline. An extension gives you an additional 2½ months to file the 5500 form. But in the case of taxpayers filing Form 5500-EZ, who obtain extensions for their federal income tax returns, and both the taxpayers and plans have the same tax year, they have the same time in which to file the retirement plan information return. In this case, a copy of the federal extension form should be attached to the Form 5500-EZ.

The type of form to be filed depends on the nature and number of participants:

- Form 5500-EZ, *Annual Return of One-Participant (Owners and Their Spouses) Retirement Plan.*
- Form 5500, *Annual Return/Report of Employee Benefit Plan.* Different schedules are attached to the return, depending on the nature and size of the plan.

No form is required if the assets in a one-participant plan have not exceeded $100,000 after December 31, 1993. A "one-participant" plan means a plan that covers, on the first day of the plan year, an owner and spouse (whether incorporated or unincorporated) or one or more partners and their spouse in a business partnership. If an owner maintains two or more plans, then total plan assets are viewed together for purposes of the $100,000 threshold.

ONLINE FILING. Forms in the 5500 series can be filed electronically, but you need special software from an EFAST-approved vendor to complete and file the return. You can see a list of approved vendors at www.efast.dol.gov.

Excise Taxes

There are a number of different excise taxes imposed by the federal government. They relate to certain fuels, luxury cars, communications, air and ship transportation, sport fishing equipment, and even bows and arrows.

Did You Know?

Prior to adoption of the sixteenth Amendment to the Constitution in 1913 permitting an income tax, federal revenue was raised entirely through excise taxes and tariffs.

Businesses that pay federal excise tax on certain fuels may have to file special returns. General information about excise taxes can be found at www.irs.gov/excise.

TAX OBLIGATIONS. Businesses that owe excise taxes must file Form 720, *Quarterly Federal Excise Tax Return*. Most federal excise taxes are due April 30th, July 31st, October 31st, and January 31st of the following year.

When you deposit excise taxes is a complex matter. Different rules—9-day rule, 14-day rule, 30-day rule, and alternative method—apply to different excise taxes. Deposit rules are explained in the instructions to Form 720.

ONLINE FILING. The IRS has introduced as new electronic filing program for excise taxes. Excise Summary Terminal Activity Reporting System or ExSTARS allows businesses to report fuel transactions online. However, businesses must make an application to participate in the ExSTARS program.

Businesses that do not file excise tax forms online can use the Internet to complete "fillable forms" online. The IRS web site contains excise tax-related forms that can be filled in and printed for signature and mailing.

PAYING FEDERAL EXCISE TAXES. Federal excise taxes can be paid through EFTPS (explained in Chapter 8 and earlier in this chapter).

Sales and Use Taxes

SALES TAX. Sales tax is a tax on the sale of an item—goods or services. It's paid by the buyer and collected by the seller who is responsible for then paying it to the taxing jurisdiction. While there is no national sales tax, more than 7,600 different jurisdictions—cities, towns, and states—within the U.S. charge a tax on the sale of goods and services. The rules vary substantially from one locality to another. Items that may be subject to sales tax in one place may be exempt in another.

The Interest Tax Freedom Act of 1998 placed a three-year moratorium on the imposition of sales tax on Internet access—such as AOL and other service providers—and on multiple or discriminatory taxation of e-commerce. This moratorium has been extended for another five years. However, the moratorium doesn't necessarily affect the imposition of sales tax on the normal sale of goods and services over the Internet. Check the laws in each state in which you do business to determine your liability for collection of sales tax.

- For developments from the Congressional Advisory Commission on Electronic Commerce, the group responsible for advising Congress on how to tax—or not tax—e-commerce, click on www.ecommercecommission.org.
- For information and analysis on emerging issues on Internet taxation, look at the Tax Cybrary at www.vertexinc.com/taxcybrary20/taxcybrary_20.html.
- For information on taxing electronic commerce, click on KPMG Peat Marwick's site at www.us.kpmg.com/salt/.

USE TAX. This is a tax imposed on buyers of in-state goods. Collection of the tax is imposed on out-of-state sellers—provided the out-of-state sellers have some connection to the state imposing the use tax. An in-state presence for purposes of this tax can be minimal—even having a product display, one sales agent, or modest inventory to meet sales needs.

Did You Know?

By 2003 it's expected that 400,000 small businesses will be selling their wares over the Internet, up from only 200 in 1996. From a tax perspective, this means more small businesses may have to file state returns they never had to file before.

CHAPTER 10

Getting Business Information and Help Online

Businesses, both large and small, routinely use computers in their business operations. If you are a business owner and have Internet connections, you can access a great deal of information to assist you in taxes, accounting, and other business matters. This information can help you run your businesses more efficiently and avoid problems with federal and state tax authorities.

In this chapter you'll learn about:

- IRS assistance for small business.
- Online accounting options.
- Offering electronic filing as a tax-free employee benefit.
- Tax-related information online.

IRS Assistance for Small Business

As part of the IRS' reorganization mandated by the IRS Restructuring and Reform Act of 1998, the IRS launched its new Small Business and Self-Employed Division (SB/SE) division in October 2000. This new division handles businesses with assets under $5 million and expects to service approximately 40 million tax filers, more than 17 million of whom are self-employed.

The SB/SE division accounts for about 40% of the total federal tax revenues collected. Headquartered in Washington, D.C., the SB/SE has service centers in Brookhaven, Cincinnati, Memphis, Ogden, and Philadelphia. The goal of this IRS division is customer assistance to help small businesses comply with the tax laws.

Toward its goal, the IRS has created a new web site (www.irs.gov/ smallbiz/index.html) to provide information on taxes for small businesses in general and help thats industry/profession specific. At the site you can link to:

- Forms and publications needed for your business. For example, you can link directly to employment tax publications.

- *E-filing*. You can connect to the latest IRS information about *e-filing* your business returns.

- STAWRS. You can link to the Simplified Tax and Wage Reporting System (see Chapter 9) to make federal and state filings easier.

- Products. You can obtain free of charge a CD-ROM Small Business Guide.

- Industry guides. The IRS has already released more than 40 audit guides that IRS personnel use to conduct audits of specific industries, such as construction and restaurants (for a direct link to these guides see www.irs.gov/bus_info/mssp/index.html). Reviewing these guides can clue you into what the IRS looks for when it audits a business in your industry. This can help your business avoid audit problems. To date, only a few such guides are linked directly to the SmallBiz site.

- Coordinated issue papers. The IRS focuses on single issues, such as meal allowances or employment contracts. Some are limited to specific industries while others apply to all businesses (for a direct link to these papers see www.irs.gov/ bus_info/tax_pro/coord.html).

- Other resources. You can link to helpful resources, a tax library, and even contact a small business expert from the IRS web site.

Online Accounting Options

You compute your taxes based on your accounting for business income and expenses. Businesses are required to keep books and

Did You Know?

The IRS accepts computer record keeping as long as you can show the applications being performed, the procedures used in each application, controls used to ensure accurate and reliable processing, and, most importantly, controls used to prevent the unauthorized addition, alteration, or deletion of retained records. The IRS also has set up guidelines for electronic imaging systems used to store receipts and other tax-related records.

records and make them available to the IRS upon request. There is no single method mandated for this purpose. More than two thirds of small business owners already use computer software, such as Quick-Books, QuickBooks Pro, and Peachtree, for record keeping instead of hand entries into account ledgers. Certainly, records maintained by computer save time and generally are more accurate than hand entries. The information stored on your computer can then be tied to tax return preparation to greatly simplify return preparation process.

Recently, there have been several online accounting products designed to supplant in-house accounting. Companies, called application service providers (ASPs), offer an alternative way to keep your books and records. These online products not only let you perform all the traditional tax and financial record-keeping available through off-the-shelf software. They also provide unique benefits:

- Much greater storage capability for your ever-growing data.
- No need for data backups and software updates (this is done automatically at the site).
- Access to books while away from the office. For example, an executive may have access to the company's online accounting information from a home computer.

Table 10.1 lists the first online accounting programs available.

CAUTION

If your business doesn't have a high-speed Internet connection, then using online software can be a frustratingly slow process. Consider using DSL, a T1 connection, or a cable modem for fast online processing.

OTHER TAX MATERIALS. In addition to books and records—your accounting system—you generally need receipts, canceled checks, and other evidence of various expenses. Whether you

TABLE 10.1 Online Accounting

PRODUCT	COMPANY	FEATURES
BAport Accounting www.baport.com	BAport Technologies Inc. 888-989-1231	$6.95/month per user. Win 95/98/Me/NT/2000; Internet Explorer 5.00.1 or later.
eLedger www.olodgor.oom	eLedger.com Inc. 877 363 3437	$19.95/month for 10 usors. Intcrnct Exploror 4.0 or later.
ePeachtree www.epeachtree.com	Peachtree Software 800-228-0068	For smaller companies. $9.99/month for 1 user ($4.95/month for each additional user). For Win 95/98/Me/NT 2000; Microsoft Internet Explorer 5.0 or later; 56Kbps Internet connection.
Intacct www.intacct.com	Intacct Corp. 877-748-7576	For larger companies (e.g., 1,000 employees) $49.95/month for 2 users ($19.95/month for 5 additional users); 10MB of online storage. Web browser other than Internet Explorer 5.5.
NetLedger www.netledger.com	NetLedger, Inc. 650-627-1000	For smaller companies. $4.95/month per user. Win or Mac; any browser version 4.0 or later. Netscape Navigator 4.06 or later or Internet Explorer 4.0 or later.

Do It Better . . .

Before opting for online accounting, make sure the product you select can perform the functions you want and need. For example, as yet, many of these products do *not* do any job costing or inventory management—features that may be essential to your type of business. If you need these features, you may have to stick with off-the-shelf software for the time being.

use an online accounting system, you must keep these other tax materials. Many small businesses simply store these materials for the period during which a return can be examined—generally three years from the due date of the return. Larger companies may use electronic imaging systems to store receipts and other tax-related records. In this case, IRS guidelines to ensure accuracy must be followed.

Online Accounting Help

Even if you don't put your books and records online, you can use the Internet to find information and assistance with your business accounting (see Table 10.2).

Offering Electronic Filing as a Tax-Free Employee Benefit

Businesses are always looking for no-cost and low-cost ways to provide added benefits to employees—to gain employee loyalty and reward staff members. You can sponsor *e-filing* of income tax returns by your employees so that they can enjoy the benefits of *e-filing*—faster refunds, accuracy, prompt acknowledgment, and e-pay options. This can probably be provided as a tax-free fringe benefit to employees as long as you offer this filing opportunity to all employees (the IRS hasn't ruled on this point yet).

Cost to Your Business

The cost of offering online filing as a fringe benefit to your employees is virtually nothing. You probably already own the computer

TABLE 10.2 Online Accounting Help

SITE	WHAT YOU CAN FIND
1-800FileTax www.filetax.com	Bookkeeping services and tax help
AccountantWeb www.accountant.org	Accounting resources
Intuit Inc. www.quicken.com/small_business	Information about accounting
IRS's Small Business Corner www.irs.gov	Information about accounting
Microsoft's bCentral www.bcentral.com	Information about accounting

equipment needed to be an *e-file* provider. Your only cost is software for preparing employee returns and software for electronic filing.

Equipment requirements for becoming an *e-file* provider for your employees include:

- IBM-compatible 486 or higher computer.
- Asynchronomous modem.
- Laser printer.
- Commercial tax software and electronic filing software.

If you need to purchase any hardware or software, it's tax deductible as an ordinary and necessary business expense according to usual tax rules.

- Computer hardware. The cost can be depreciated over five years. Alternatively, the cost can be expensed up to $24,000 in 2001 (up to $25,000 in 2003).
- Software. While most software must be depreciated over three years, tax preparation software is fully deductible in the year of purchase—its useful life is limited to one year.

Of course, when your computers are in use for *e-filing* they may not be available for other business applications. It generally takes 15 minutes to an hour to file a single return, depending upon its complexity. You can, of course, schedule *e-filing* after normal business hours since *e-filing* can be done 24-hours a day.

POTENTIAL LIABILITY. If you offer this fringe benefit, can you be held liable for errors or other problems on employee returns? No. As an *e-file* provider, you aren't liable for any preparation errors in employee returns. You aren't liable for any preparer penalties with respect to employee returns. Only the person who signs the return—the employee (and possibly a paid preparer)—is responsible for the accuracy and validity of the information.

Tax-Related Information Online

Your ability to claim certain deductions can involve judgment calls on your part. Fortunately, you can turn to the Internet for some guidance to help you formulate a decision. You can also use the Internet to find information that can help you meet your tax obligations on both the federal and state levels.

Reasonable Compensation

What should you pay your employees? The answer isn't as simple as what you can afford to pay. You need to stay competitive so you'll attract and retain valuable workers—especially in a tight labor market.

But there's a tax ramification to knowing what the going rate is for a particular job description. The reason: Businesses can deduct only *reasonable compensation*. The tax law doesn't set a dollar amount on what's reasonable—you must decide given all the facts and circumstances of your situation—job responsibility, location of the business, etc. But one way to help you determine what's reasonable compensation is to look at what similar businesses are paying for comparable work. You can find this information at:

- Salary.com (www.salary.com). This site provides pay scales for jobs in different metropolitan areas and states.

- CareerInfoNet (www.acinet.org). Lists salaries and benefits in various locations throughout the country.

- National Association for Compensation Benefits and Total Rewards (www.worldatwork.org). This site provides surveys on skill-based pay, incentive pay, bonuses, and other benefits.

Classifying Workers as Employees or Independent Contractors

If you're not the only worker in your company, you need to determine whether your help are employees or independent contractors. If they're employees, you're responsible for employment taxes (discussed in Chapter 9). If they're independent contractors, you must file information returns reporting payments to them (also discussed in Chapter 9).

You want to be sure to make the right decision on worker classification. This is the number one audit target of the IRS. The reason: It's easier for the IRS to collect employment taxes from business owners than from the workers themselves. If you classify them as independent contractors and the IRS successfully reclassifies them, you can be liable for substantial interest and penalties. What's more, your employee benefit programs—medical coverage and retirement plans—could be placed in jeopardy because you failed to include these workers in the plans.

You can see what factors the IRS uses to classify workers by viewing the IRS at www.irs.gov/prod/bus_info/training.html.

Travel and Entertainment Expenses

Travel and entertainment (T&E) expenses are common to most businesses. It's also an area in which the IRS looks closely to make sure you're entitled to the write-offs you claim. You can minimize problems in this regard if instead of paying the actual cost of travel, you reimburse employees using standard government rates—referred to as per diem rates. Per diem rates cover the cost of lodging, meals, and incidental expenses. Using per diem rates eliminates the need to substantiate the cost of travel—the per diem rate is assumed to be that cost.

Per diem rates are fixed by the federal government according to its fiscal year beginning on October 1st. From your perspective, you have two sets of per diem rates within each calendar year—one for the first three quarters of the year and another for the final quarter of the year.

You can find a listing of per diem rates for business travel at:

- IRS (download IRS Publication 1542, *Per Diem Rates*, from www.irs.gov).
- Policyworks (www.policyworks.gov).

Charitable Contributions of Excess Inventory

Want to get a write-off for inventory that isn't moving? Consider donating it to charity and claiming a charitable contribution deduction. Generally, write-offs are limited to your cost. But C corporations can claim an enhanced deduction (the property's adjusted basis, which is usually cost, *plus* one-half of its unrealized appreciation—but no more than 200% of the property's basis) for donations of:

- Computer equipment to schools (grades K–12) and libraries. *Note:* This enhanced deduction is set to expire on December 31, 2003, unless Congress extends it.

Do It Better . . .

You can opt to use both sets of per diem rates for the year—one for January 1 through September 30 and the other for October 1 through December 31. Or, you can opt to use the rates effective on January 1st for the entire year—no IRS election form need be filed (just use the old rates when claiming your travel deduction).

- Property, including inventory, donated to a charity for the care of children, the ill, or the needy.

- Donations of scientific property used for research by certain educational institutions or scientific research organizations.

For some businesses, one difficulty in taking advantage of this potential write-off is finding the appropriate charity. Here's where the Internet can help you. Check out a donations clearinghouse to find a match for your inventory items. These clearinghouses include:

- Gifts in Kind International (www.giftsinkind.org or 703-836-2121).

- National Association for Exchange of Industrial Resources (www.hvacmall.com/listing/naeir.htm or 800-562-0955).

Self-Employed Individuals

Sole proprietors face unique tax issues as self-employed individuals. There are things they must do—such as pay enough estimated tax to cover their self-employment tax obligations. There are things they can't do—such as write-off all of their health insurance costs as a business deduction.

For tax information geared to the self-employed, see About.com (http://taxes.about.com/money/taxes/bl_se.htm).

Multistate Operations

If you do business in more than one state, the complexity of your operations increases. You have to contend with the tax rules in each location for:

- Income taxes.
- Employment taxes.
- Sales and use taxes.
- Property taxes.

To help you understand the tax rules in different states—or to find the answer to a specific question on state taxation, click on the Deloitte & Touche Center for Multistate Taxation (www.uwm.edu/Dept/Business/MSTax/SALT).

Using the Internet for Tax Planning

CHAPTER 11

What the IRS Web Site Can Offer You

The IRS often has the reputation of being anti-taxpayer—them against us. But following the IRS Restructuring and Reform Act of 1998, the IRS issued a new mission statement:

> Provide America's taxpayer's top quality service by helping them understand and meet their tax responsibilities and by applying the tax law with integrity and fairness to all.

Toward this end, the IRS maintains a state-of-the-art web site full of "top quality" taxpayer assistance. The site is continually updated with developments, new taxpayer services, and added information.

The IRS web site (www.irs.gov) is one of the most widely visited sites on the Internet, getting more than 1.5 billion hits between January 1, 2001, and April 16, 2001—the tax filing season for 2000 returns. There's good reason for the site's popularity. It provides a great deal of easy-to-use information and assistance to individuals, businesses, and tax professionals.

Of course, the IRS site isn't the only place you'll find important and helpful tax information. Integrated throughout this chapter and covered in greater detail in the next chapter, you'll find references to other educational or commercial sites to help you track down tax material and information to help you get things right or just do it better.

In this chapter you'll learn about:

- Finding material for tax preparation.
- Doing tax research at the IRS site.
- Solving your tax questions online.
- Keeping up to date.

Finding Material for Tax Preparation

Whether you use commercial software (online or off-the-shelf) or a paid professional to prepare your return, the more you know about taxes the better off you'll be. You may be able to take steps throughout the year that will translate into tax savings when you prepare your return. If you use a tax professional, your understanding of tax matters and things you must do can cut down on professional fees. Or you may have a tax problem you need an answer to. In order to gain an understanding of taxes or find an answer to your problem, you need to know how to find tax materials, tax information, and tax advice online.

Fortunately, you can find the material you need to learn about taxes and prepare your returns through the Internet. And perhaps the best site for this is the source—the IRS web site (www.irs.gov or ftp.irs.gov). Here you can find:

- Tax forms—for the current year and prior years. You can even see draft versions of forms for the upcoming year. Also find forms at Re: Quest dot Net (www.re-Quest.net/financial/taxes/taxforms/index.htm).
- Instructions to tax forms (where the instructions are not part of the forms themselves).
- Tax publications—prepared by the IRS in plain language on nearly 100 subjects for both individuals and business owners.

A listing of the most commonly used publications at the IRS web site is found in Table 11.1.

Don't know which form or publication to download? Let's say you want to know about deducting dental fees you paid for your child's braces? You can search for publications at the IRS web site by

TABLE 11.1 IRS Publications

PUBLICATION NUMBER	PUBLICATION TITLE
1	Your Rights as a Taxpayer
3	Armed Forces' Tax Guide
4	Students' Guide to Federal Income Tax
15	Circular E, Employer's Tax Guide
15A	Employer's Supplemental Tax Guide
15B	Employer's Tax Guide to Fringe Benefits
17	Your Federal Income Tax
51	Circular A, Agricultural Employer's Tax Guide
54	Tax Guide for U.S. Citizens and Resident Aliens Abroad
225	Farmer's Tax Guide
334	Tax Guide for Small Business
378	Fuel Tax Credits and Refunds
463	Travel, Entertainment, Gift, and Car Expenses
501	Exemptions, Standard Deduction, and Filing Information
502	Medical and Dental Expenses
503	Child and Dependent Care Expenses
504	Divorced or Separated Individuals
505	Tax Withholding and Estimated Tax
508	Tax Benefits for Work-Related Education
509	Tax Calendars for 2001*
510	Excise Taxes in 2001*
514	Foreign Tax Credit for Individuals
520	Scholarships and Fellowships
521	Moving Expenses
523	Selling Your Home
524	Credit for the Elderly or the Disabled
525	Taxable and Nontaxable Income
526	Charitable Contributions
527	Residential Rental Property (including Rental of Vacation Homes)
529	Miscellaneous Deductions
530	Tax Information for First-Time Homeowners
531	Reporting Tip Income

(Continued)

TABLE 11.1 *(Continued)*

PUBLICATION NUMBER	PUBLICATION TITLE
533	Self-Employment Tax
536	Net Operating Losses (NOLs) for Individuals, Estates, and Trusts
537	Installment Sales
538	Accounting Periods and Methods
541	Partnerships
542	Corporations
544	Sales and Other Dispositions of Assets
547	Casualties, Disasters, and Thefts
550	Investment Income and Expenses
551	Basis of Assets
552	Record Keeping for Individuals
553	Highlights of 2000 Tax Changes*
554	Older Americans' Tax Guide
555	Community Property
556	Examination of Returns, Appeal Rights, and Claims for Refund
559	Survivors, Executors, and Administrators
560	Retirement Plans for Small Business
561	Determining the Value of Donated Property
564	Mutual Fund Distributions
575	Pension and Annuity Income
583	Starting a Business and Keeping Records
584	Casualty, Disaster, and Theft Loss Workbook
587	Business Use of Your Home (including Use by Day-Care Providers)
590	Individual Retirement Arrangements (IRAs) (including SEP-IRAs and SIMPLE IRAs)
595	Tax Highlights for Commercial Fishermen
596	Earned Income Credit
721	Tax Guide to U.S. Civil Service Retirement Benefits
907	Tax Highlights for Persons With Disabilities
911	Direct Sellers
915	Social Security and Equivalent Railroad Retirement Benefits

TABLE 11.1 *(Continued)*

PUBLICATION NUMBER	PUBLICATION TITLE
919	How Do I Adjust My Tax Withholding
925	Passive Activity and At-Risk Rules
926	Household Employers Tax Guide
929	Tax Rules for Children and Dependents
936	Home Mortgage Interest Deduction
939	General Rule for Pensions and Annuities
946	How to Depreciate Property
950	Introduction to Estate and Gift Taxes
954	Tax Incentives for Empowerment Zones and Other Distressed Communities
967	The IRS Will Figure Your Tax
968	Tax Benefits for Adoption
969	Medical Savings Accounts
970	Tax Benefits for Higher Education
971	Innocent Spouse Relief
972	Child Tax Credit
1212	List of Original Issue Discount Instruments
1542	Per Diem Rates
1544	Reporting Cash Payments of Over $10,000

*These publications are updated annually. For example, Publication 509 will be updated for Tax Calendars in 2002.

topic—medical expenses—or by keyword—dental fees. Just click on the search feature at the bottom of the IRS home page and enter the keyword (or words). In this way you'll find IRS Publication 502, *Medical and Dental Expenses*, and Schedule A of Form 1040, *Itemized Deductions*.

Do It Better . . .

Want your tax education in small doses? The IRS can help you learn about taxes—step by step—during the tax filing season. Get a free daily tax tip at www.irs.gov/prod/news/nandf.html.

Doing Tax Research at the IRS Site

The tax law is highly complex. But you don't have to be an Einstein to find an answer to your tax question. All you need is a basic understanding of how the tax law is set up and where on the IRS site or elsewhere on the Internet to look for answers.

The starting point for federal tax law is comprised of the Internal Revenue Code—the tax law enacted by Congress. It's now about 1,395,000 words.

The next layer of tax law is Treasury regulations—rules issued by the Treasury to explain sections of the Code. As of June 2000, there were about 20,000 pages of regulations, made up of more than 8 million words. It's enough to make your head spin. You'll find web sites for the Internal Revenue Code listed in the next chapter.

You can find Treasury regulations at IRS (www.irs.gov/tax_regs/index.html)—for a plain language version of the regulations. There are also some plain language versions of proposed regulations—regulations that have been issued in a type of draft form to allow tax professionals to comment on them before they are finalized.

As further interpretation of tax law, court decisions can provide guidance. Of course, not all courts agree on a particular question, but you can look at what's been decided so far. Court decisions aren't listed on the IRS web site—you must use sites for the courts, law schools, or other sites that routinely publish court decisions. For example, you'll find cases interpreting federal tax law from the following U.S. courts:

- Tax Court at www.ustaxcourt.gov. You can find all cases decided after 1998. You can also see Tax Court rules—for example, how to bring a "small case" (one involving a tax up to $50,000) without a lawyer in an expedited procedure for only a $60 court filing fee. You can also find Tax Court rules at UncleFed's Tax Board (www.unclefed.com).
- District courts (www.taxresources.com).
- U.S. Claims Court (www.taxresources.com)
- U.S. Supreme Court at (www.supremecourtus.gov).

Courts aren't the only authorities interpreting the tax law. The IRS also weighs in on what it believes Congress intended as the meaning for a particular law. The IRS issues administrative rulings:

Did You Know?

While Letter Rulings are IRS interpretations of the law, legally they aren't viewed as precedent—something you can rely on as a definite IRS position (unless you're the party who requested the ruling). They're responses to questions posed by specific taxpayers—in effect private rulings. However, they do serve as indications of IRS thinking on a particular subject.

- Revenue Rulings.
- Revenue Procedures.
- Notices.
- Announcements.
- Letter Rulings.
- General Counsel Memoranda.
- Actions on Decisions.
- Technical Advice Memoranda.

IRS rulings are posted online weekly in the Internal Revenue Bulletins (www.irs.gov/bus_info/bullet.html). Twice a year these IRS rulings are republished in the Cumulative Bulletin (CB) and, once republished, the IRS no longer posts the old Internal Revenue Bulletins. So, if you're looking for older rulings, look to the CBs.

Private letter rulings, AODs, and other informal pronouncements aren't easy to find at the IRS web site. However, you can gain access—if you know what you're looking for—through the IRS's Freedom of Information Act office (www.irs.gov/prod/news/efoia/irs-online.html). *Note:* There's no index to the materials found at this site—you have to know the number of the IRS pronouncement you're looking for. And not every letter ruling or other informal pronouncement is available here.

Solving Your Tax Questions Online

You may have a specific tax question—during the tax season or at any other time of the year. If you have a tax question, you don't necessarily have to pay for expert advice. You may be able to find an answer on your own—online. There are numerous tools at the IRS web site you can use in your search for an answer to your tax question.

Basic Questions and Answers

Want to understand certain tax fundamentals? Then use the IRS's online interactive sessions, called Tax Trails, to delve into specific tax topics (www.irs.gov/ind_info/tax_trails/index.html). For example, you can click on "Can you deduct business use of the home expenses?" to see if you're eligible for a home office deduction. Or you can click on "Do you have to use Form 8615 to figure your child's tax?" to learn about the kiddie tax for children under the age of 14.

You can also call the IRS's TeleTax Topics by phone at 800-829-4477 to hear prerecorded messages on approximately 150 tax topics. You can find a listing of topics in the instructions to your tax return.

INNOCENT SPOUSE RELIEF. If you file a joint return, both spouses are jointly and severally liable for all of the tax (plus any interest and penalties) relating to the return. But if one spouse believes that the other is responsible for an underpayment of tax, he or she can request innocent spouse relief. You can check your eligibility for this relief at the IRS web site by clicking on "Spousal Tax Relief Eligibility Explorer" under "Tax Info for You."

E-mailing the IRS

If you've done your research but don't have an answer to your question, you can call the IRS for help at 800-829-1040—you may or may not get through. And once you get past the busy signal, the wait can be up to an hour or more—especially at tax time. But you don't have to use your phone to get a personal response to a question. You can e-mail the IRS (www.irs.gov/help/newmail/user). Submit your question as clearly as possible. Then wait for a response by e-mail. The

Did You Know?

You can try calling the IRS with your question at 800-829-1040. But according to the General Accounting Office, only about one-quarter of calls are answered. If you do get through, you can probably get a satisfactory response to basic questions—for example, which form or schedule to use in reporting certain income or claiming certain write-offs. Otherwise, you're better off researching the question on your own—or using the assistance of a tax professional.

Did You Know?

You can't always rely on IRS advice. The Treasury Inspector General's Office says that the IRS answers incorrectly 49% of the time—about 50% of the time for walk-in questions at IRS offices—and provides insufficient answers for 24% of all queries. So if you get an answer to your question from the IRS, be sure to note the name of the IRS employee and his or her employee number who responded to you. This can help you avoid penalties if you rely on the IRS advice, which turns out to be incorrect and your return is later questioned.

response isn't instantaneous—it may be days before you get your answer—if you hear back at all.

Appealing IRS Decisions

Even though IRS audit rates are at an all-time low, you may still be one of the unfortunate few to have your return questioned. If the IRS says you owe additional taxes, you don't have to agree and pay up. You can appeal an initial IRS determination.

So if you've received an adverse IRS decision—for example, on appeal the IRS says you owe more than you believe is correct—you have certain rights of appeal. You can bring your case before the IRS Appeals Office who will review your case independently from the office that made the initial adjustment to your taxes.

LEARN YOUR RIGHTS. As a taxpayer, you have certain rights in the appeal process. You can find out about your rights online by downloading the following IRS publications:

- Publication 1, *Your Rights as a Taxpayer*.
- Publication 5, *Your Appeal Rights and How to Prepare a Protest If You Don't Agree*.

Do It Better . . .

You aren't required to have representation—an accountant, attorney, or other tax professional—when you bring your appeal. Using IRS publications as guides, you can pursue your own appeal. But if the amount in dispute is substantial or you just don't feel up to the task, it may pay to pay for help.

> ## Do It Better . . .
>
> Don't rely solely on what the IRS tells you your rights are as a taxpayer. Commercial sites can provide valuable information about your rights and help you resolve your tax problems. For example, at TaxHelpOnline you can ask an expert or attend an online seminar (www.taxhelponline.com).

- Publication 556, *Examination of Returns, Appeals Rights, and Claims for Refunds*.
- Publication 1660, *Collection Appeals Rights*.

FAST TRACK APPEALS. The IRS is now testing a program that will allow you to bring your appeals to mediation. This is a dispute resolution program in which third parties (not exclusively IRS personnel) help to work out a settlement of the matter. At present, the test involves only large taxpayers—those with adjustments in issue of $1 million or more. But if the program is successful it may be expanded to other taxpayers. Visit the IRS site for news updates on the fast track appeals program.

ALTERNATIVE DISPUTE RESOLUTION. In addition to the mediation program, the IRS is also testing various other programs to resolve taxpayer disputes in a faster, fairer, and cheaper way. Some of these other programs include:

- Arbitration. Under a test program, eligible taxpayers may request that their case be handled by binding arbitration. Only factual issues—not legal issues—can be presented in this forum.
- Early referral request. Under another test program, taxpayers who believe that they are wasting their time in the Examination or Collection Division can move one or more unresolved issues directly to the Office of Appeals—saving time and money.
- Expanded settlement authority. Case managers handling initial examinations have been given greater authority to accept settlement offers in certain situations.

Visit the IRS site for any developments on the alternative dispute resolution program.

Resolving Problems in an Emergency

If you've tried to fix tax problems—for example, a lost refund or a miscredited tax payment—but have been unsuccessful so far, don't give up hope. Help is just a few clicks away. The IRS Problem Resolution Office (PRO) is designed to handle just these matters.

As part of the PRO, the IRS Taxpayer Advocate Service, is given the authority to solve problems that have eluded a satisfactory outcome despite repeated efforts on the part of taxpayers. The Taxpayer Advocate Service, headed by a National Taxpayer Advocate, is supposed to be there to protect your rights as a taxpayer. You can contact PRP by calling 877-777-4778. Or click on www.irs.gov/ind_info_advocate.html.

When is it time to turn to the PRO for help? Consider asking for assistance in these situations:

- You have experienced a delay of more than 30 days in resolving your issue.
- You haven't received a response or a resolution by a promised date.
- You'd suffer irreparable injury or long-term adverse impact.
- You're facing an immediate threat of adverse impact.
- You'll incur significant cost (including professional fees for representation).

The Taxpayer Advocate can also help in emergency situations—to stay a levy or seizure that's about to occur. File Form 911, *Application for Taxpayer Assistance Order (ATOA)*. The form can be downloaded from the IRS site or you can even ask an IRS employee to complete one for you over the telephone. You can fax in your Form 911 to your local Taxpayer Advocate. To qualify for immediate assistance, you must show that you are suffering (or will suffer) a significant hardship if the IRS proceeds with its actions. Generally, any IRS action is suspended while the Taxpayer Advocate investigates your situation. The Taxpayer Advocate can then resolve your case administratively.

When you contact the Taxpayer Advocate, be prepared to provide the following information:

- Your name, address and Social Security number (or employer identification number if applicable).
- Your telephone number and the hours you can be reached there.

- The type of tax return—for example, Form 1040—and the tax year or years involved.

- A description of your problem and what you've already done to try to resolve it (including the office you've already contacted).

- A description of the hardship you're facing if this applies to you.

To find a local Taxpayer Advocate, look at IRS Publication 1546, *The Taxpayer Advocate Service of the IRS*, which you'll find at the IRS web site.

Keeping Up to Date

The tax law is constantly changing. In June of 2001, a tax package providing $1.35 trillion in tax cuts over 10 years was signed into law—creating new opportunities for taxpayers in 2001 and in years to come.

And not a day goes by that there isn't some other new development—a court case, an IRS ruling, or even new legislation from Congress. How are you supposed to stay up to date? There's no easy way. The amount of information can be overwhelming. Even tax professionals can find it difficult if not impossible to stay on top of every tax development.

But you have some ways of learning about what's new in taxes—especially major developments. The IRS web site contains several ways to help you keep up on what's new in taxes:

- Digital Dispatch—an online publication from the IRS highlighting key developments. More specifically the Digital Dispatch can alert you to new forms and publications, key filing dates, new IRS news releases and announcements, and new developments on the IRS web site. Sign up to receive your copy via e-mail at www.irs.gov/help/newmail/maillist.html. All you have to do is provide your e-mail address—no name or other personal information is required. There is a similar on-line publication at the IRS web site for state and local tax developments.

- IRS Publication 553, *Highlights of 2000 Tax Changes*—download this publication to see what's new for individuals and businesses. The IRS updates this publication each year, so early in 2002 you can find an updated version for 2001 changes (www.irs.gov/hot/index.html).

TABLE 11.2 Getting Updated Tax Information

SITE	WHAT YOU'LL FIND
SecureTax.com (www.securetax.com)	Tax newsletters and other information
TaxAnalysts (www.tax.org)	Daily tax news
Tax Digest (www.taxdigest.com)	Subscribe to this electronic publication (receive issues via e-mail)
Taxware International (www.taxware.com/news/newsinfo.htm)	News and information

- Instructions to tax returns. At the front of the instructions to the return you'll find a "What's New" section.
- Draft versions of tax forms. The IRS posts drafts of tax forms months before the final versions are printed. By viewing the drafts you can see what's new in tax returns well before you actually have to prepare them. The draft versions can be found by clicking on Taxes for Business and then on Tax Professionals.

Tax professionals who want continuing education credits can take part in an interactive series sponsored in part by the IRS (www.taxtalktoday.org). The cost for continuing education credit is $25—those who simply want to participate in the series without the credit can do so for free.

Commercial Sites with Free Updates

You don't need to rely solely on the IRS to keep you up-to-date on tax developments. There are a number of commercial sites—some general and some devoted to specific tax areas—that can help you stay abreast of tax news. (See Table 11.2).

Online Tax Research

Have a tax question but don't want to engage a tax expert? You may be able to find the answer yourself—online. The Internet has a vast array of tools and resources that you can tap into for assistance with your tax questions. In Chapter 11 you can see how the IRS web site provides a vast array of research tools to help you find your answers. But you aren't limited to researching tax questions at the IRS site. There are many commercial sites as well as other government, university, law school, and tax-exempt organization sites that provide research assistance for tax matters.

Online tax research can help you resolve issues you're currently facing or learn about planning ideas to help you go forward.

In this chapter you'll learn about:

- Using tax web browsers.
- Online chats and other tax forums.
- Doing tax research online.
- Learning from online tax guides.
- Learning from major accounting firms.
- Locating tax professionals online.

Using Tax Web Browsers

Have a tax question or problem and don't know where to begin? Or are you looking for a particular tax resource and are at a loss on how to start your search? Then use one of several tax web browsers that can provide you with numerous links to specific tax sites. Table 12.1 represents a partial list of tax browsers you can use to link up with the tax information you're looking for.

CAUTION

Be wary of tax advice you learn at chat rooms and online forums. Remember that the tax information you obtain here may not always be correct—it may be only one person's opinion and that person may not necessarily be a tax professional—even though some professionals are regular participants in these forums.

Online Chats and Other Tax Forums

While online chat rooms have a reputation as a dating forum, they can be a great place to exchange ideas about taxation. Participation is free. And your identity remains anonymous so you don't have to be concerned about posing personal tax questions.

E-MAIL GROUPS. Some professional groups and universities host online discussions on specialized tax topics. You can join a group and then submit questions by e-mail. A moderator then organizes questions and answers and sends results to group members via e-mail. For a listing of tax discussion groups of this type, click on the search engine by the University of Chicago Law

TABLE 12.1 Tax Web Browsers

NAME	URL
About.com	http://taxes.about.com/money/taxes/mbody.htm
El.com (Essential Links to Taxes)	www.el.com/dir/cat_taxes.asp?tree=126
Excite	www.excite.com/apple/guide/Money/Taxes/
iFigure	www.ifigure.com/money/taxes/taxes.htm
Tax Resources	www.taxresources.com
TaxUp	www.taxup.com
TaxWeb	www.taxweb.com

Lists at www.lib.uchicago.edu/cgi-bin/law-lists (click on "tax" to find groups focusing on this topic).

NEWSGROUPS. Online "conversation"—with the ability to submit questions and receive immediate responses—are available at a number of sites. Some are moderated by a tax professional—making things a little more organized. Other sites are free-for-alls.

- Misc.taxes (http://misc.taxes.moderated) is a chat room devoted to the topic of taxes—with the added structure of a tax professional who acts as the moderator.

- Tax logic (www.taxlogic.com) lets you submit tax questions which are answered by a tax professional—all questions and answers are then posted on a message board.

- ThatHomeSite (www.thathomesite.com/forums/taxes) is a forum for posting tax questions—all questions and answers are posted, and follow-up responses to your questions can be e-mailed directly to you.

To find other chat rooms for taxes, use your basic web browser "News and Message" function or click on Uchats (www.uchats.com). Some web sites, such as Office.com (www.office.com), have run chat rooms on tax issues for the tax season only (February through April 15th).

Doing Tax Research Online

Government web sites—for example, the U.S. Tax Court or the IRS site—aren't the only places to find tax cases and ruling online. If you want to do some tax research on your own, a number of universities and commercial sites can connect you with current and prior cases and rulings—for free. You no longer have to travel to your local courthouse or law school to find this information. Table 12.2 lists some good research sites.

Do It Better . . .

To search for messages that have already been posted at certain newsgroups, click on DejaNews (www.deja.com).

TABLE 12.2 Online Research Sites

SITE	WHAT YOU'LL FIND
Dennis Schmidt's State and Local Taxes (www.taxsites.com/state.html)	Links to state tax information
FindLaw.com (www.findlaw.com)	U.S. Supreme Court decisions, other cases, and regulations.
Jurisline.com (www.jurisline.com)	Internal Revenue Code and regulations
Legal Information Institute at Cornell Law School (www.4.law.cornell.edu/uscode/26/) (www.law.cornell.edu/opinions.html)	Internal Revenue Code Decisions from federal and state courts
LexisONE (www.lexisone.com)	Decisions from federal courts (this Lexis access is free but there's a subscription charge for more extensive Lexis research)
TaxNet USA, Inc. (www.taxnetusa.com)	Property tax information—by location
TaxTopic.com (www.taxtopic.com)	Online research portal for federal and state taxes
TaxUp (www.taxup.com)	State tax information—by location
Taxweb (www.taxweb.com)	Links to tax information
Touro Law School (www.tourolaw.edu/AboutTLC/Courts)	Information about and decisions from federal courts
TRAC, a data-gathering organization associated with Syracuse University (http://trac.syr.edu/tracirs)	Check your risk of being audited, based on your income, location, and other factors
U.S. Tax Code Online (www.fourmilab.ch/ustax/ustax.html)	Internal Revenue Code

Do It Better . . .

Don't know exactly where to go? Try a helpful government portal (www.firstgov.gov) to find links to state and local government.

Commercial Sites

In addition to government information, there's a lot of good information out there on commercial web sites. In some cases, however, you may have to pay for access or information. Some sites to consider:

- Boardroom Inc. (www.bottomlinesecrets.com/taxes)—articles about tax developments and strategies.
- BWideas.com (www.bwideas.com)—this author's web site, providing monthly tax-related ideas for business owners and individuals.
- CCH Inc. (http://Onlinestore.cch.com)—tax news and information, including descriptions of breaking tax legislation.
- Research Institute of America (RIA) (www.riatax.com)—tax news and information.

Learning from Online Tax Guides

Perhaps the premier tax guide is the IRS' own Publication 17, *Your Federal Income Tax*. It contains all the basic information about personal income tax returns and provides references to other IRS publications that can furnish you with more details on a specific topic. You can download this guide from the IRS web site—or you can simply view it there.

Several commercial sites now have online tax guides to provide you with general tax information. They are generally written in easy-to-understand language and contain not only tax explanations but also planning ideas. Table 12.3 lists some sites to consider.

Learning from Major Accounting Firms

Many accounting firms today have a presence on the Web. Some sites are purely promotional—listing firm members, areas of spe-

TABLE 12.3 Online Tax Guides

GUIDE	URL
Bloomberg Tax Guide	www.bloomberg.com/money/tax
SmartMoney.com Tax Guide	www.smartmoney.com/tax
Tax Harbor Tax Guides	www.taxharbor.com

cialization, and contact information. Other sites provide tax information that may be beneficial to you—for personal taxes or in business. For example, within days of enactment of the Economic Growth and Tax Relief Reconciliation Act of 2001—sweeping federal tax legislation containing more than 400 changes in the Internal Revenue Code—each of the major accounting firms as well as numerous other firms had posted extensive explanations and analysis of the new law.

The "Big Five" Firms

If you want to engage an accountant in one of the largest accounting firms, known as the "big five," you can find an office near you by clicking on the firm's web site. Even if you don't engage one of these firms to assist you in your tax matters, you can use the site to gain valuable information about tax developments and links to other tax sites (see Table 12.4).

Other Firms

Tax help from CPAs isn't limited to the big five firms. Many smaller firms, including solo practitioners, maintain web sites that can offer you helpful information about your taxes. Table 12.5 gives a sampling of what you can find at the sites of these accounting firms.

TABLE 12.4 Accessing the "Big Five" Accounting Firms

FIRM'S SITE	WHAT YOU'LL FIND
Arthur Andersen (www.arthurandersen.com)	Information for business on e-commerce/other information
Deloitte & Touche LLP (www.dtonline.com)	Developments affecting federal, state and local taxes
Ernst & Young (www.ey.com)	Breaking tax news (also click on the Knowledge Center for Tax Resources)
KPMG Peat Marwick (www.us.kpmg.com/services/tax/index.html)	Links to other tax sites
Pricewaterhouse Coopers Lybrand (www.taxnews.com)	Tax news

TABLE 12.5 Getting Help and Information from Accounting Firms

FIRM'S SITE	WHAT YOU'LL FIND
David Berdon & Co., LLP (www.dberdon.com)	Articles on personal finance and taxes
Grant Thornton (www.gt.com)—click on Resources	Resources on financial institutions; state and local taxes
TaxMama (www.taxmamma.com/IRSnews)	Online newsletter

Locating Tax Professionals Online

There are a number of different types of professionals who can help you with your taxes—from preparing your returns to helping you fight the IRS in an audit or on appeal. These professionals include:

- Attorneys specializing in tax law.
- Certified public accountants (CPAs).
- Enrolled agents (authorized to practice before the IRS).
- Public accountants.

The type of professional you select depends on your tax task or problem and what you're willing to pay. Naturally, the more skilled the professional, the higher the cost of assistance. Fees vary considerably in different locations—highest in large metropolitan areas. But when large tax dollars are at stake or criminal charges are or may be pending, the cost of qualified assistance certainly justifies the cost.

UNDERSTANDING YOUR RIGHT OF PRIVACY TO TAX INFORMATION. Keep in mind that the information you divulge to your tax professional may not necessarily be privileged. The law recognizes a broad privilege for communications between an attorney and client. But there's only a limited privilege between federally authorized tax practitioners (other than attorneys) and their clients. (Federally authorized tax practitioners are individuals who can practice before the IRS.) This client-tax practitioner privilege only applies to tax advice given in limited circumstances and only with respect to the IRS. It doesn't apply to:

Do It Better . . .

When there's any concern about confidentiality, be sure to engage an attorney. If necessary, the attorney can hire an accountant to work with him or her on your matter and that work remains privileged—the accountant is your attorney's agent.

- Tax return preparation.
- Criminal matters.
- State tax matters (unless your state is one of about 17 states that recognize full or partial accountant-client privilege).
- Written communications to corporate officers of tax shelters.
- Waivers of privilege, including disclosures of information to third parties.
- Tax matters concerning other agencies or regulatory bodies (such as the SEC or state boards of accountancy).

ACCOUNTANTS.   When you looked for a doctor in your neighborhood, you probably asked your neighbor or friend for a referral. The same approach can be applied to finding an accountant. You can use word-of-mouth to find an accountant in your area to help you with your tax matter. Ask family, friends, business associates, local merchants or others for a name and phone number.

If you can't get a referral to a CPA in this way, then look in your local phone directory under "accountants-certified public." Or contact your State Society of CPAs to find referrals to an accountant in your area.

But you also have another alternative for finding an accountant in your locality—you can go online for referrals. Some sites to check for referrals to accountants include:

- American Institute of CPAs—AICPA (www.aicpa.org) can provide you with a listing of its members in your area.
- CPAdirectory (www.cpadirectory.com) lets you search the country—by name, city and state—to find a specific CPA. Or you can find a listing of CPAs within a particular zip code.

Your local phone directory also contains listings to public accountants under "accountants-public" and to enrolled agents under accounting and bookkeeping-general services (look for those who have the enrolled agent designation).

You aren't necessarily limited to an accountant in your city or town. Today you don't have to sit down with an accountant to have your tax returns prepared by this professional. You can use an accountant online to prepare your return—regardless of where you're located. For example, you can find an accountant who will prepare your return within 48 hours and file it online—for as little as $75.

LAWYERS. Perhaps the best way to find legal assistance is by referral—from family, friends, or business associates.

If you don't have a referral to an attorney, you can certainly find one to help you. You can, of course, use the old way—checking listings in your local phone directory. Or you can call your local bar association (listing in the telephone directory) for several referrals to attorneys with specialties or expertise in taxation. But online resources can make your search easier. These include:

> **CAUTION**
>
> Make sure the attorney you contact is a tax professional. The lawyer who handled your house-closing or divorce or drafted your will may not be the best person to handle your tax matters.

- AttorneyFind (www.attorneyfind.com) is a legal referral site.
- Respond.com (ww2.lawyers-respond.com) is a legal referral site.
- Lawyers.com (www.lawyers.com), by Martindale-Hubbell (publisher of a guide to lawyers), is the most comprehensive online search for an attorney anywhere in the country. You can search by specialty to find an attorney to handle your tax matter.
- MyCounsel.com (www.mycounsel.com) is a legal referral site.

OTHER TAX PROFESSIONALS. CPAs and attorneys aren't the only tax professionals who may be able to help you. Enrolled agents are individuals who've passed an IRS test authorizing them to practice before the IRS.

To find a tax professional, click on:

- Internet Directory of Tax Professionals (www.tax-directory.com)
- National Association of Tax Professionals (www.taxprofessionals. com).

Other Online Resources

Looking for legal assistance online? There's now a host of sites to help you find the answers you seek—many at no cost. (See Table 12.6.)

TABLE 12.6 Online Help Resources

SITE	WHAT YOU'LL FIND
IRS.com (www.irs.com)	Ask an expert your tax questions
Law.freeadvice.com (www.law.freeadvice.com/tax_law)	Tax advice
MyLawyer.com (www.mylawyer.com)	Legal information
Nolo.com (www.nolo.com)	View topics
Taxlogic (www.taxlogic.com)	Ask a tax professional a question and receive an answer within 24 hours—for free
USLaw.com (www.uslaw.com)	Online chats with an attorney for $9.95 per 30-minute session (or $24.95 annual subscription fee)

CHAPTER 13

Online Tax Planning

Taxes aren't something you do once a year. You need to think about the tax implications of each and every transaction you make—so you can minimize your taxes to keep more of your hard earned dollars as well as to simplify tax return preparation at the end of the year.

Tax planning is an ongoing process. You're never "finished" with planning—you continually refine your decisions and make new ones as needed. Today there are many online resources to help you with tax planning throughout the year, not only with income tax planning but also with tax planning for your investments, saving for college for your children or grandchildren, planning for your retirement and, finally, planning for your estate.

In this chapter you'll learn about:

- Income tax planning.
- Investment planning.
- College savings planning.
- Retirement planning.
- Estate planning.

Income Tax Planning

General Tax Planning

If you think you paid more than you should have this year, don't wait until you file your return next year to make changes. Take steps now that can translate into tax savings on next year's return. Learn what you must do—or not do—to reduce your taxes.

For example, if you didn't have enough deductions to itemize this year, you may be able to use a basic tax strategy, called "bunching," to enable you to itemize next year. Under this strategy, you plan to make discretionary deductible expenditures—such as charitable contributions—in one year to boost your itemized deductions for that year. The following year, you simply take the standard deduction. You then alternate this approach to bunch deductions (and itemize) in one year, while claiming the standard deduction in the next year.

INDIVIDUALS. For general tax planning information for individual income taxes, click on:

- H&R Block (www.hrblock.com/taxes/index.html)—go to tax planning.
- MSN's MoneyCentral Taxes (http://moneycentral.msn.com/tax/home.asp)—go to tax planning.
- TaxPlanet.com (www.taxplanet.com)—go to Year-Round Tax Guide.
- Yahoo Tax Center (http://taxes.yahoo.com/).

BUSINESSES. For general tax planning information for small business owners, click on:

- Entrepreneur Magazine (www.entrepreneur.com).
- Inc.online (www.inc.com).
- Office.com (www.office.com).

Alternative Minimum Tax (AMT)

This is a tax designed to compliment the regular tax to ensure that all taxpayers—regardless of write-offs they can otherwise claim—will pay at least some income tax. There is an AMT for individuals and an AMT for C corporations (other than "small C corporations" which are exempt from AMT).

Originally the AMT was aimed at high-income taxpayers who were

Did You Know?

It's estimated that about 1.5 million individuals already pay AMT and this number could rise to as many as 35 million by 2010 unless the law is changed. The reason: AMT brackets and exemptions aren't indexed for inflation and the reduction in the regular income tax makes the AMT more pronounced.

able to avoid the regular income tax with tax shelter investments and other write-offs. Today, the AMT hits an ever-increasing circle of moderate and even lower income taxpayers who deduct certain items to reduce their regular tax that are not deductible for AMT purposes. For 2002 through 2004 there's some tax relief because the exemption amounts for AMT purposes have been increased slightly, but after 2004 more individuals may fall into the AMT trap.

The AMT can be a highly confusing area of the tax law, even for tax-savvy individuals. You probably have a feel for whether you'll owe tax or get a refund even before you complete your return. But it's virtually impossible to eyeball whether or not you'll have any AMT liability. You need to run the numbers. You can do this using tax preparation software at tax time. Or you can use an online calculator to make your projections at any time during the year (www.smart-money.com/tax/capital/index.cfm?story=amt).

If you want to plan around the AMT, you'll want to keep track throughout the year of your potential exposure. To do this, you need a good grasp of what the AMT is all about—so you can spot potential traps. For example, you'll want to know which special items or deductions can trigger the AMT—for instance, large miscellaneous itemized deductions and state and local taxes, which are *not* deductible for AMT purposes. And you'll want to know what impact the exercise of your incentive stock options can have on AMT.

You can learn about the AMT at:

- General Accounting Office (www.gao.gov/new.items/ggoo180.pdf) —ask for report DDG-00-180.
- IRS (www.irs.gov)—Publication 17, *Your Federal Income Tax*. *Note:* To date there is no separate IRS publication on the AMT.

Charitable Deductions

Americans are very generous people. According to IRS statistics released in 2001 for 1998, deductions for contributions were about

Did You Know?

Most tax professional organizations support the repeal of the AMT. However, Congress seems reluctant to go this far and opted in 2001 for a quick fix for the short run. It remains to be seen whether repeal will gain support before millions more Americans fall into the AMT trap.

$109.2 billion (and other sources estimate that the figure was more than $143 billion in 2000). The average gift exceeded $3,200.

Individuals and businesses can deduct contributions of cash and property to charitable organizations. The limits on donations by individuals and C corporations differ. These rules can be found in IRS Publication 526, *Charitable Contributions*, that you can download from the IRS web site.

CAUTION

Gifts of $250 or more must receive a written acknowledgment from the charity—a canceled check is not considered proof of the donation. Property donations exceeding $5,000 ($10,000 for non-publicly traded securities) must be accompanied by a qualified appraisal. No appraisal is required for donations of publicly traded securities.

CHECKING ON TAX-EXEMPT ORGANIZATIONS. First and foremost, you can only claim a charitable contribution deduction if you give to an organization that has received tax-exempt status from the IRS. You can't necessarily rely on an organization's claim that donations to it will be tax deductible—tax-exempt status can change at any time.

The IRS publishes a list of exempt organizations in Publication 78, *Cumulative List of Organizations*. You can use an online database—the electronic version of Publication 78—to search for exempt organizations under legal names or recognized abbreviations (such as "VFW") (www.irs.gov/prod/bus_info/eo/eosearch.html).

MAKING DONATIONS ONLINE. You can, of course, send a check in the mail to benefit your favorite charity. But today you can make charitable contributions online—by charging them to your credit card. Using this online method can be especially helpful at the end of the year. Donations charged by December 31st are treated as made in the year even though you don't pay the charge bill until the following year.

Do It Better . . .

Donations made in 2001 are worth more in tax savings than they would be if made in 2002. The reason: Tax rates decline in 2002, making deductions less valuable at that time than they are in 2001.

Today more than 600,000 charitable organizations participate in an online donation program:

- Charitygift (www.charitygift.com).
- DonateTo.com (www.DonateTo.com).
- Guidestar (www.guidestar.org).

Be sure to check for any donation minimums or other restrictions when making your gift.

DONATING COMPUTERS OR CELL PHONES. If you're upgrading your computers or cell phones, don't throw away your old ones—donate them. You can donate your old equipment to charity—and get a tax benefit for your good act. If you don't know an organization that can use your old things, contact:

- Computers for Schools Association (www.detwiler.org).
- Computers for Youth (www.cfy.org).
- Donate a Phone (www.donateaphone.com).
- National Cristina Foundation (www.cristina.org).
- PEP's National Directory of Computer Recycling Programs (www.microweb.com/pepsite).

For special rules on computer donations by C corporations see Chapter 10.

Did You Know?

It's been estimated that by 2004 there will be 315 million obsolete computers. But if yours is a 486 or Macintosh PowerMac, iMac, or newer, there's an organization or individual out there who can put it to good use.

DETERMINING THE VALUE OF DONATED PROPERTY.   When you give items to charity, you need to know the item's current fair market value. The amount of your deduction for long-term gain property (such as stock held more than one year) is its fair market value. The deduction for short-term gain property is limited to your cost. The amount of your deduction for household goods and cars is the lesser of your cost or value. Generally, fair market value means the price that a willing buyer would pay to a willing seller if all the facts of the item were disclosed. But how do you know what this is? To help you deduct value, you can use certain online sites:

- IRS (www.irs.gov)—see IRS Publication 561, *Determining the Value of Donated Property*.
- Kelley Blue Book (www.kbb.com)—for determining the value of used cars.
- UsedComputer.com (www.usedcomputer.com)—for determining the value of old PCs.

Investment Planning

Information on Investing

Investing is a complex topic, involving many considerations—an understanding of investment options, a determination of your investment goals and risk tolerance, and of course, the tax implications of your investment decisions. Fortunately, the Internet contains a myriad of sites that can address each of these aspects of investment.

For general information about the tax implications of investing, click on:

- GE Center for Financial Learning (www.financiallearning.com).
- SmartMoney.com (www.smartmoney.com).

Capital Gain and Loss Planning Online

Capital gains and losses are one of the most confusing areas in the tax law. The reason: There are multiple capital gains tax rates—different rates apply depending upon your how long you've owned the asset that's been sold, the tax rate on your other (ordinary) income, and the type of asset that's been sold. Just a glance as Schedule D, *Capital Gains and Losses*, reveals the complexity of this area of the tax law.

You can't make effective investment decisions until you know the tax implications of your actions. So before you can start to plan and make effective tax decisions, you need a solid understanding of the tax rules for capital gains and losses. You need to know about:

- Holding period—how long you've owned the asset.
- Basis—what you paid or some other amount for determining gain or loss.
- Short-term—assets held one year or less.
- Long-term—generally assets held more than one year. Most assets held more than one year are taxed at no more than 20%. But starting in 2001 there is an even more favorable tax rate for assets held more than five years—18% (and for those in the 10% or 15% tax bracket the tax rate is just 8%). *Note:* To qualify, taxpayers other than those in the 10% or 15% tax bracket on ordinary income must acquire the assets after 2000 or a special election must be made in 2001 to treat the assets as having been sold and re-acquired at the start of the year.

If you don't think you're fluent in this basic tax lingo for investments, then you need an elementary or refresher course on capital gains and losses. You can find the information you need in various IRS publications that you can download from the IRS web site:

- Publication 544, *Sales and Other Distributions of Assets*.
- Publication 550, *Investment Income and Expenses*.
- Publication 551, *Basis of Assets*.
- Publication 564, *Mutual Fund Distributions*.

You can also find basic information about capital gains and losses at the web sites listed in Table 13.1.

Tracking Investments

When you acquire shares in a corporation or mutual fund at different times and different prices and later sell only part of your holdings, you have an opportunity to control your gain or loss. The tax law gives you different ways to determine which shares are being sold so you can minimize your gain or maximize your loss—as needed for your overall tax picture. Your options:

- First-in first-out (FIFO) method. You are assumed to have sold the first shares you acquired. This method automatically applies

TABLE 13.1 Web Sites with Strong Basic Information

TAX SITE	WHAT YOU'LL FIND
CNNfn (http://cnnfn.cnn.com/markets/ personalfinance/	Advice on investing
Fairmark (www.fairmark.com	Free tax guide for investors
Money (www.money.com)	Articles from Money magazine on investments
MoneyCentral (www.msn.com/moneycentral)	General investment information, including rules on capital gains and losses
Motley Fool (www.fool.com or AOL keyword: fool)	General investment information, including rules on capital gains and losses
Quicken.com (www.quicken.com/investments)	Basic information about capital gains and losses—free
Smartleaf Advisor (www.smartleaf.com)	Free calculator for determining when to take a loss (online advisory service at $20/month)
Women's Wire (www.womenwire.com/money)	Advice on investing geared toward single women

unless you select another method for determining which shares you've sold.

- Average cost method. In this case you average the cost of all your mutual fund shares in a particular fund and then divide by the number of shares. When you sell part of your holdings, you get an average basis for those shares for purposes of determining your gain or loss. This method can *only* be used for mutual fund shares—not for individually owned stocks. You can refine the average cost method by using a double category to divide

Example

You bought 100 shares of X Corp. on each of the following dates: May 1, 1999, June 1, 2000, and July 1, 2001. On March 1, 2002, you sell 250 shares of X. You are assumed to have sold 100 shares acquired on May 1, 1999, 100 shares acquired on June 1, 2000, and 50 shares acquired on July 1, 2001.

your shares into long-term and short-term categories and using the averages for each category.

- Specific identification method. This method lets you select exactly which shares you wish to sell. You must give written instructions to your broker or mutual fund company on precisely which shares you're selling and receive written confirmation of your order. It is not certain—the IRS hasn't confirmed it—but some tax experts suggest that a written standing order to a mutual fund or broker to *always* sell first the shares with the highest cost basis, may satisfy this written instruction requirement.

Remember—your option to use the average cost method and the specific identification method instead of defaulting to the FIFO method depends on good record keeping. You can keep paper records of your stock and mutual fund shares. You'll find a mutual fund share record-keeper in IRS Publication 564, *Mutual Fund Distributions*, which you can download from the IRS web site.

Or you can use various online tracking programs to log in purchases and sales of stocks and mutual fund shares.

- Mutual fund companies. Many now keep track of this information for you and let you view your information online.

- AmericaOnline (click on "Quotes"). You can keep track of your holdings by inputing purchase information. But you can't refine your records to reflect multiple purchase dates.

- Gainskeeper (www.gainskeeper.com) can be used to alert you when to sell by providing a grading system for your holdings. Cost: $49 to $299/year.

Mutual Fund Sites

Today almost half of U.S. households own mutual funds—a key investment for both retirement plans and personal savings.

Example

Same facts as above but instead you wish to sell all of the shares acquired on July 1, 2001, 75 shares acquired on June 1, 2000, and 75 shares acquired on May 1, 1999. You give instructions to your broker to execute this sale and receive a written confirmation of your order.

RECORD KEEPING.   Mutual funds today are more helpful in keeping track of your basis in the funds—information you need to determine gain or loss when you sell your holdings. For example, the funds now include dividend reinvestments in your basis. If you fail to include this amount in your basis, you wind up paying tax on the same money twice—once when you receive the dividend or capital gain distribution from the fund, and a second time when you sell your shares and pay more gain than you need to (because of underreporting your basis).

You can, of course, rely on the fund to keep track of your investments, reinvestments, and sales. But you can also do this record keeping yourself. If you don't want to maintain paper records, your other alternatives include:

> **CAUTION**
>
> If you use computer software or online sites to keep track of your fund holdings, it's a good idea to print out your information—at least at key times (year-end, quarterly, etc.) or backup the information onto disk or other backup method. This will protect you if your online information becomes corrupted or is lost.

- Personal financial software (for example Quicken or Microsoft Money).

- Online recordkeepers (for example, America Online).

If you have a large number of transactions throughout the year—for example, you do a lot of online trading—you may want to use special online products to keep track of your transactions and simplify your tax return preparation:

- GainsKeeper (www.gainskeeper.com)—online tracking of transactions. Cost: $49 for up to 100 trades; $299 for unlimited trades.

- TradersAccounting.com (www.tradersaccounting.com)—MS Excel spreadsheet that can be used as an attachment to Schedule D.

TAX EFFICIENCY.   For mutual funds held in tax-deferred accounts, such as IRAs, 401(k) plans, or SIMPLE plans, fund managers can buy and sell their holdings without any immediate tax impact on you. But for funds held in your personal accounts, turnover by fund managers can directly impact your taxes. For example, fund profits can translate into capital gain distributions to you—even if the value of your fund has declined.

This concern about fund turnover is called tax efficiency. Knowing a fund's tax efficiency can help you decide whether to hold the funds in tax-deferred accounts or personal accounts. To check on the tax efficiency of your fund or those you are thinking about acquiring, click on:

- Morningstar (www.morningstar.com).
- PersonalFund.com (www.personalfund.com/index.html).
- SEC Mutual Fund Calculator (www.sec.gov/mfcc/mfcc-int.htm).

Stock Options

You may receive stock options from your employer. There are different types of stock options—incentive stock options (ISOs) and nonqualified stock options. The tax rules vary with the different types of stock options (see Table 13.2).

The Internet can help you manage your stock options—learning what they're all about and figuring their worth (see Table 13.3).

Municipal Bonds

Municipal bonds usually have lower coupon rates than taxable bonds with comparable maturities. The reason: The interest on municipal bonds is free from federal income tax and may also be state free so municipalities can pay less while still attracting investors. If you buy a municipal bond, you may keep more in bond interest on an after-tax basis than with a taxable bond with a comparable maturity. For example, if you are in a 40% tax bracket (federal and state combined) and earn 4.5% on a 10-year municipal bond that's exempt from your federal and state income tax, you'd have to receive more than 7.5% in interest on a 10-year taxable bond to have a higher return.

To compare the return on municipal bonds to that of taxable bonds for your tax bracket, click on InvestingInBonds.com (www.investinginbonds.com).

College Savings Planning

One of the single largest expenses that any family may face is paying for a college education for a child. Today, the four-year cost at top institutions is about $150,000. According to the National Commission on the Cost of Higher Education, tuition alone rose from $2,881 to $15,581 a year at private universities for the period of 1976 to 1996—a 440% increase compared to a rise in the median household income of only 82% during this same time frame. No one can predict what

TABLE 13.2 Tax Treatment for Employees and Employers

TAX TREATMENT	ISOS	NONQUALIFIED STOCK OPTIONS
When granted	No tax	Taxable if the value of the option is readily ascertainable and substantially vested
Exercise	No regular tax; spread between the value of the stock and the amount paid is an adjustment for alternative minimum tax purposes	Taxable as ordinary income if option not subject to tax at time of grant
Deduction by employer	No deduction at time of grant, exercise or sale (if sale occurs more than 2 years from grant and 1 year from exercise); deduction for amount of ordinary income recognized by employee if sale within 2 years of grant or 1 year of exercise	Deduction for amount of ordinary income recognized by employee

TABLE 13.3 Stock Options Sites

SITE	WHAT YOU'LL FIND
MyStockOptions.com (www.mystockoptions.com)	Explanation of the tax rules on stock options and valuation methods
SmartMoney.com (www.smartmoney.com/tax/capital/ index.cfm?story=options)	Stock option calculator

the cost will actually be in 10 years or more. But one thing's for certain—it's going to be considerably higher.

If you have children or anticipate having them and want to plan now for their higher education, it's helpful to make projections on what you'll need to save. For general college savings calculators:

- Fidelity College Cost Calculator (www100.fidelity.com).
- NASD Investor Services Calculators (http://investor.nasd.com/ gamec/default.html/).

- T. Rowe Price College Cost Calculator (www3.troweprice.com/cftools/CPC/index.cfm).
- USA Today.com Calculators (www.usatoday.com/money/calculat/mcfront.htm).

Tax Incentives for Higher Education Savings

The tax law encourages you to save for college in several ways:

- Coverdell Education Savings Account—contributions up to $500 in 2001 and $2,000 starting in 2002 can be made for beneficiaries under age 18 (or for a special needs beneficiary without regard to age). Earnings are tax-deferred and withdrawals used for qualified education expenses are tax free. Starting in 2002, tax-free withdrawals can be made not only for higher education purposes but also for the payment of grades K–12—both public and private school.
- U.S. savings bonds—interest on bonds acquired after 1989, which are used to pay qualified higher education expenses, is tax free if certain conditions are met.
- State tuition programs—earnings on contributions are tax deferred (this is explained below). (Starting in 2002 distributions from these plans for qualified educational expense will be tax free. Further, private institutions can offer prepaid tuition plans but not savings programs).

You can find out about federal tax incentives for higher education in IRS Publication 970, *Tax Benefits for Higher Education*, at the IRS web site.

529 Plans

To help families save for the high cost of a college education for their children, states can set up two types of college savings plans

- Tuition prepayment plans—contributions of set amounts are guaranteed to cover the cost of tuition, regardless of how it may be increased. A number of states offer prepayment plans. And starting in 2002, private institutions—colleges and universities—can also offer these prepayment plans in which you purchase tuition certificates or prepay tuition on behalf of a beneficiary.
- 529 plans (named after the section in the Internal Revenue Code creating them)—savings plans that can be used to cover college

costs. Contributions are managed by the state or money managers it selects (such as Fidelity or TIAA-CREF). All states (other than Georgia and South Dakota) now offer these savings plans. The plans are set up in the name of a beneficiary, but the contributor essentially retains control over the funds, even being able to tap into them—although there's an IRS penalty of 10% on withdrawals other than for the beneficiary's higher education expenses.

You can learn about different programs through the program managers:

- Fidelity (www.fidelity.com).
- TIAA-CREF (www.tiaa-cref.org).

You can also learn about 529 plans at state-specific web sites. For example, New York maintains a site for its program (www.nysaves.org).

Retirement Planning

Retirement can be a significant portion of your life—lasting 20 years, 30 years or more. Financially, you want to make sure that you have enough money to live on for your retirement years—without having to make significant adjustments to your standard of living.

The Internet can help you plan for your retirement, providing you with information about general retirement planning concerns, Social Security, retirement plans and IRAs, and more.

General Retirement Planning

Planning for retirement income involves a comprehensive approach to three key areas: Social Security, pensions and retirement plans,

Did You Know?

You don't necessarily have to be a resident of a state to contribute to its 529 plan. Thus, you can shop around the country for plans offering the best investment options with the lowest withdrawal penalties. However, state income tax deductions may be only available to residents of the state in which the plan operates.

and personal savings. For general retirement planning information, click on:

- Charles Schwab (www.schwab.com)—go to Planning.
- CNNfn (http://cnnfn.cnn.com/markets/personalfinance)—go to Retirement Planning.
- Quicken (www.quicken.com)—go to Business News and Money News.

Social Security Benefits

While you can't rely on these benefits to provide you with a comfortable retirement, they can be a significant part of your retirement income. Each year, about two months prior to your birthday, you should receive by mail a personal earnings and benefits statement prepared exclusively for you by the Social Security Administration (SSA). This statement shows what you've paid into the Social Security system and what you can expect to receive in the way of benefits if you retire at age 62 (the earliest retirement age), your normal retirement age (currently age 65 but increasing to 67), and age 70 (the delayed retirement age). If you retire before your normal retirement age, your Social Security benefits are permanently reduced—the reduction amount depends on just how early you retire. If you postpone retirement until age 70, you'll receive credit for your added working years.

Alternatively, you can use an online calculator from SSA to project your benefits (www.ssa.gov/retire). Here you can alter the variables—your earnings and when you expect to retire—to see what you would receive as monthly benefits.

Saving for Retirement

In order to have a financially secure retirement, you can't rely solely on Social Security benefits. You need to be able to tap into both retirement

Did You Know?

Someone in the United States turns age 50 every 55 seconds. Baby boomers are poised to start retiring in about 10 years—so retirement planning should be of great interest. Especially since one recent survey showed that about half have saved less than $50,000 so far.

accounts—personal IRAs as well as company-sponsored plans—and personal savings to provide you with the income you'll need.

IMPACT OF INFLATION.   One of the biggest variables in what you need to save for retirement is inflation. This eats into the buying power of your retirement dollars. For example, if inflation runs at 4% annually (it was 3.4% in 2000), the buying power of a dollar is cut in half over 18 years (the historic inflation rate has been just a little over 3%). To see the impact that inflation can have on your money, look at a special inflation calculator at the U.S. Bureau of Labor Statistics (www.bls.gov).

General savings calculators include the following:

- Finan Center (www.financenter.com/index_page.html).
- KJE Computer Solutions Financial Calculators (www.dinky town.net).
- NASD Investor Services Calculators (http://investor.nasd.com/ gamec/default.html/).

Retirement savings calculators include the following:

- Bloomberg (www.bloomberg.com)—click on Retirement.
- Finan Center (www.financenter.com/index_page.html).
- KJE Computer Solutions Financial Calculators (www.dinky town.net).
- NASD Investor Services Calculators (http://investor.nasd.com/ gamec/default.html/).
- Smart Money (www.smartmoney.com/tax/)—click on retirement savings.
- USA Today (www.usatoday.com/money/calculat/mcfront.htm).

SAVINGS BONDS.   If you own U.S. Savings bonds—Series E, EE, or I— that you plan to spend as retirement income, you'll want to know how much they're worth. You can find redemption value information at the Bureau of Public Debt's web site (www.savingsbonds.gov/sav/ savcalc.htm).

Be sure to remember that if you've been deferring tax on savings bond interest, you'll owe tax on the interest portion of the proceeds when you cash in the bonds. The only way to avoid this tax result:

- Use the proceeds from Series E, EE, or I bonds to pay qualified higher education costs for yourself, spouse, or dependent and meet certain income limits as mentioned above.

- Roll over Series E or EE bonds into HH bonds. These are savings bonds that pay interest semi-annually. You'll pay tax on the HH bond interest—but you'll defer tax on all of the built-up interest on the original savings bonds until the HH bonds reach their final maturity date—20 years after acquisition.

Record keeping for your bonds can become a burden—you may own numerous bonds for many years. But you can keep track of your savings bond holdings by downloading a wizard from the savings bond web site (www.savingsbonds.gov/sav/savwizar.htm).

Roth IRA Conversion Calculators

Roth IRAs are attractive retirement savings vehicles. The reason: Earnings in a Roth IRA become tax free if left in the account for at least five years and aren't tapped until after age 59½ or on account of death, disability, or buying a first home (tax-free limit here is $10,000). What's more, there are no required lifetime distributions from Roth IRAs so if you don't need the money for retirement income, you can leave your Roth IRA to heirs as a substantial inheritance. And, starting in 2002, those age 50 and older may be eligible to make additional "catch-up" contributions to their accounts.

If you have a traditional IRA, you may wish to convert it to a Roth IRA. But the cost of conversion is paying tax on the conversion amount—what you would have paid had you taken the converted amount as a distribution from your traditional IRA. The entire amount must be reported as ordinary income in the year you make the conversion (only IRAs converted in 1998 were subject to a four-year spread of the resulting income).

Does it pay for you to convert? You have to weigh the current tax cost against the future potential for tax-free income. Can you convert? You must meet eligibility requirements—your adjusted gross income (without regard to the conversion amount) can't exceed $100,000. And it only makes sense to convert if you have the funds to pay the resulting tax—it doesn't make sense to deplete the IRA for the taxes due.

You can use an online calculator to help you assess the feasibility of making a conversion. Such calculators include:

- T. Rowe Price (www.troweprice.com/tools/toolsInsight/Home. html).
- Vanguard (www.vanguard.com/cgi-bin/RothConv).

New Law Contribution Options

The 2001 tax law raised the contribution limits for IRAs and elective deferrals to 401(k) plans, 403(b) annuities, SIMPLE plans, and other elective deferral programs. The limits are phased in over several years starting in 2002. And additional "catch up" contributions can be made by those age 50 and older at the end of the year.

These new contribution limits greatly increase your ability to save for a financially secure retirement—but you need to know your options and make choices. You can learn about the new contribution limits created by the 2001 tax law at the web sites of each of the Big Five firms (see Chapter 12) as well as at:

- CCH Inc. (www.cch.com).
- RIA (www.ria.com).

Taking Company Pensions

When you retire, companies may offer you a choice on your retirement benefits: receive a monthly pension or take a lump-sum distribution of those benefits. The choice isn't easy—it's difficult to know which alternative will prove to be the better choice. This is especially true if you're married and have joint and survivor options to consider.

But the Internet can help you with your decision. To find professional assistance in making your decision, look for a financial planner who specializes in this type of advice. Or you can contact:

Do It Better . . .

If you converted your IRA to a Roth IRA this year but the value of the account has declined, you may wish to consider a recharacterization—putting the money back into the traditional IRA. You'll avoid paying income tax on the higher value of the account at the time of conversion. You'll then have to wait until next year to attempt a conversion again—only one conversion per year is permitted.

- The Pension Rights Center (www.pensionrights.org or 202-296-3776).

FIGURING REQUIREMENT MINIMUM DISTRIBUTIONS FROM QUALIFIED RETIREMENT PLANS. You must start to take distributions from 401(k) and other company-sponsored retirement plans when you turn age 70½. You can postpone distributions until your actual retirement from the company if later than this age (but this postponement can't be used by those who own more than 5% of the company).

If you fail to take minimum required distributions (MRDs), you can be subject to a 50% penalty. To figure your MRDs, see the rules that follow for IRAs.

Figuring Required Distributions from IRAs

In order to make sure you don't outlive your retirement funds, you probably want to take as little as possible from retirement plans, using up personal savings first. This lets money in retirement plans continue to build-up on a tax-deferred basis.

But the tax law requires you to start withdrawals from traditional IRAs by the end of the year in which you attain age 70½ (although the first can be postponed until April 1st of the following year). You must take at least the minimum required distribution (MRD) in order to avoid a 50% penalty. But how do you know much your MRD should be?

You can find the rules for MRDs, including the table you need to figure distributions, in IRS Publication 590, *Individual Retirement Arrangements*, at the IRS web site.

For general information about MRD planning and other IRA topics, click on:

- Natalie B. Choate, Esq. (www.ataxplan.com/articles_fr/dist_rules.htm).

Do It Better . . .

If you're unmarried but have someone you wish (or need) to benefit, it's probably wiser to opt for the lump-sum distribution. Otherwise, your pension ends when you do—at death the plan has no obligation to make any further payments, regardless of how much or how little of the pension you actually collected.

- Seymour Goldberg, Esq., CPA (www.goldbergira.com).
- Robert Keebler's (www.rothirs.com).
- Ed Slott's IRA Help (www.irahelp.com).

Estate Planning

Federal estate taxes are being phased out over the next 10 years—but if you die within this time period before repeal becomes effective, your estate may still face an estate tax. It's helpful to understand what you're up against so you can plan according.

Estate Planning Information

If you own property and have people you're concerned about after your death, you need to do some estate planning. This will ensure that your property is disposed of according to your wishes and that the people you care about are protected—without regard to whether there are any estate taxes involved.

But from a tax perspective, if your holdings are more than modest, you also need to be concerned about the tax bite that can erode the assets you leave to your heirs. You need to plan now to reduce or eliminate the estate tax that may be due. You can't rely on simply living long enough to see repeal take effect. And even if you do live to 2010, the following year, the estate tax comes back into effect as if repeal had never happened.

Your estate is comprised of all property you have an interest in at the time of your death. This includes assets you own solely in your name and assets you jointly own (your share is included in your estate).

DEATH TAXES. Currently there is a federal estate tax on estates valued at the time of death at more than the exemption amount (see Table 13.4).

Did You Know?

Those whose estates are valued at $1 million or less will no longer need to think about federal estate taxes after 2001. The exemption amount rises to $1 million in 2002 and increases in stages thereafter. In 2011, when the estate tax resumes following one year of repeal, the exemption amount is again $1 million unless repeal is made permanent.

TABLE 13.4 Exempt Amount for Federal Estate Tax

YEAR	EXEMPTION AMOUNT
2001	$675,000
2002–2003	$1 million
2004–2005	$1.5 million
2006–2008	$2 million
2009	$3.5 million
2010	No estate tax
2011	$1 million

States may have their own death taxes—in the form of a state estate tax or a state inheritance tax (an estate tax is imposed on the estate—managed by an executor or other personal representative—while an inheritance tax is imposed on heirs who receive property on account of death).

Many states limit their death tax to the amount of the federal credit for state death taxes. However, this credit is reduced in stages in 2002 through 2004 and ceases after 2004. States may enact new state death taxes to recoup the revenues lost by the change in the federal estate tax rules. Check your state's web site for its current rules as well as changes the state may make in its death tax laws (see Chapter 5).

If the value of your assets today exceeds $1 million, you should estimate your federal estate tax liability so that you can plan to reduce it. You can use an online tax calculator for this purpose:

- Banksite.com (www.banksite.com/calc/estate).
- Bloomberg (www.bloomberg.com).
- Estate Web! (www.estateweb.com/common/calc.htm).
- Fidelity (http://web400.fidelity.com/legacy/index.htm).

Glossary

ACH credit method Payment through a financial institution under EFTPS.

ACH debit method The direct payment method under EFTPS.

acknowledgment Proof in the form of an electronic file stamp that your return has been accepted by the IRS as filed.

adjusted gross income Gross income less above-the-line deductions (such as IRA contributions and alimony payments).

Alaska Permanent Fund dividend An annual dividend payment to residents of Alaska who timely file for the dividend.

application service providers (ASPs) Companies offering online accounting applications such as bookkeeping and information storage.

apportionment A formula for allocating the amount of taxes that must be paid to each state in which a company does business.

authorized private carrier A company designated by the IRS for delivering tax returns to the IRS which qualify for the timely-sent timely-mailed rule.

authorized service provider   A company designated by the IRS to process a tax payment by credit card.

average cost method   Method of determining which mutual fund shares are being sold when shares were acquired at different times, and less than all of the shares are being sold.

backup withholding   Withholding on interest and dividends at the fourth lowest individual income tax rate if the recipient's Social Security number provided to the payer is incorrect.

basis   What you paid for an asset or some other amount for determining gain or loss when the asset is sold.

confirmation number   Proof that your payment of tax by credit card has been processed.

convenience fee   The amount paid to commercial companies who oversee the payment of taxes by credit card.

cookies   A file placed on your hard drive to allow a web site to monitor your use of the site.

customer service number (CSN)   The five-digit number provided on the IRS TeleFile package to identify the taxpayer.

direct debit   A method for paying your taxes by authorizing that funds be taken from your checking or savings account.

direct deposit   A refund method in which the amount is deposited directly in your bank account.

EFAST   ERISA Filing Acceptance System used to process information returns for employee benefit plans.

e-file   Electronic filing for tax returns and other forms.

e-file **provider**   A paid preparer who can submit your return to the IRS electronically for a fee.

EFTPS   The Electronic Federal Tax Payment System, a tax payment and reporting system of the U.S. Treasury.

electronic return originator (ERO)   See *e-file* provider.

ExSTARS   The Excise Summary Terminal Activity Reporting System that allows businesses to report fuel transactions online.

federally authorized tax practitioners   Individuals who can practice before the IRS.

FIFO   First-in first-out; a method for determining which shares are being sold when such shares were acquired at different times, and less than all of the shares are being sold.

fillable forms   Forms that can be filled in online but which must be downloaded for mailing.

holding period   The time an asset has been owned.

import   Bring in data from another source (see integration).

I-file   See *e-file*.

installment agreement   A method for paying your taxes over time.

intangibles tax   A tax on stocks, bonds, and other securities levied by Florida on its residents.

integration   Bringing in data from another source (see import).

jurat statement   The portion of the return in which a taxpayer agrees that, under penalty of perjury, the information contained in the return is correct.

long-term   Owning an asset for more than one year.

NetFile   See TeleFile.

Net-file   See *e-file*.

nexus   A connection with a state—generally a physical presence—that forms the basis for requiring the filing of a state tax return.

offer in compromise   An arrangement with the IRS in which you are allowed to pay less than the full amount of tax owed because of severe financial hardship.

overpayment   Paying too much in taxes so that a refund is owed to you.

paid preparer   A person or company who prepares tax returns for a fee and/or files returns electronically for a fee.

paperless returns   Returns containing electronic signatures (such as self-select PINs) for which no paper signature forms, W-2 forms, or other paper attachments are required.

PC-file   See *e-file*.

refund anticipation loan   A short-term loan based on the amount owed to you as a tax refund.

routing number   The nine-digit number used to identify your financial institution when making direct deposits of tax refunds.

Secure Socket Layer (SSL)   Industry standard encryption technology used to protect your personal information online.

self-select PIN   A five-digit number picked by the taxpayer to be used as an electronic signature for tax returns.

short-term   Owning an asset for one year or less.

specific identification method   Method of determining which shares are being sold when shares were acquired at different times, and less than all of the shares are being sold.

statute of limitations   The period during which you can file a claim for refund or the IRS can examine your return and assess additional taxes.

tax efficiency   Turnover in mutual funds giving rise to tax results.

taxable income   Income after reduction by personal exemptions and the standard deduction or itemized deductions; income on which tax is figured.

telefile   A method for preparing and filing a simple tax return using a telephone.

underpayment   Paying too little in taxes so that amounts are owed.

v-file   See *e-file*.

web-file   See *e-file*.

Directory of Online Tax Web Sites

Chapter 1

SITE	WHAT YOU'LL FIND
IRS (www.irs.gov)	Tax forms, publications, *e-file*, news and more (see specific listings in other chapters)

Chapter 2

SITE	WHAT YOU'LL FIND
2nd Story Software	Information about TaxAct Deluxe
AARP (www.aarp.org/taxaide)	Locations nationwide of free tax preparation and filing assistance
CompleteTax (www.completetax.com)	Online tax preparation site
Eopinions.com (www.eopinions.com/finc-Taxes)	Rating of tax preparation software
esmartTax.com (www.eSmartTax.com)	Online tax preparation site
ezTaxReturn.com (www.eztaxreturn.com)	Online tax preparation site

SITE	WHAT YOU'LL FIND
H&R Block TaxCut (www.taxcut.com_)	Online tax preparation site
H.D. Vest (www.myhdvest.com)	Online tax preparation site
Intuit (www.intuit.com)	Information about TurboTax, TurboTax Deluxe, TurboTax for Home and Business
Kiplinger's TaxCut (www.taxcut.com)	Information about TaxCut Deluxe
PC Magazine (www.zdnet.com/pcmag)	Rating of tax preparation software
Quick-Tax.com (www.quick-tax.com)	Online tax preparation site
Social Security Administration (SSA) (www.ssa.gov)	To change or update Social Security card information (e.g., name change)
TaxACTOnline.com (www.taxact.com)	Online tax preparation site
TaxBrain.com (www.taxbrain.com)	Online tax preparation site
Taxes4less.com (www.taxes4less.com)	Online tax preparation site
TurboTax for the Web (www.quicken.com/freedom)	Online tax preparation site

Chapter 3

SITE	WHAT YOU'LL FIND
AARP (www.aarp.org/taxaide)	Explanation of VITA program
IRS (www.irs.gov/elec_svs/ss-pin.html)	Locating an *e-file* provider (including exemplary *e-file* providers)
IRS (www.irs.gov/ind_info/coll_stds/collect.html)	Information about installment payment agreements
IRS (www.irs.gov)—click on "Forms and Pubs"	Downloadable current and past-year forms and instructions; fill-in forms
Official Payments Corporation (www.officialpayments.com)	Charging taxes online
PhoneCharge, Inc. (www.About1888ALLTAXX.com)	Charging taxes online
Social Security Administration (SSA) (www.ssa.gov)	To change or update Social Security card information (e.g., name change)

Chapter 4

SITE	WHAT YOU'LL FIND
IRS (www.irs.gov)—click on "Forms and Pubs"	Downloadable current and past-year forms and instructions; fill-in forms
Official Payments Corporation (www.officialpayments.com)	Charging taxes online
PhoneCharge, Inc. (www.About1888ALLTAXX.com)	Charging taxes online

Chapter 5

SITE	WHAT YOU'LL FIND
CompleteTax (www.completetax.com)	Online tax preparation site for state income taxes
FileYourTaxes.com (www.FileYourTaxes.com)	Online tax preparation site for state income taxes
H&R Block Online (www.hrblock.com)	Online tax preparation site for state income taxes
Kiplinger Tax Cut (www.taxcut.com)	Online tax preparation site for state income taxes
MyHDVest (www.myhdvest.com)	Online tax preparation site for state income taxes
ON-LINE 1040A (www.quick-tax.com)	Online tax preparation site for state income taxes
Tax Act (www.taxact.com)	Online tax preparation site for state income taxes
TaxBrain (www.taxbrain.com)	Online tax preparation site for state income taxes
Tax-Engine.com (www.tax-engine.com)	Online tax preparation site for state income taxes
TaxSlayer (www.taxslayer.com)	Online tax preparation site for state income taxes
TurboTax for the Web, TurboTax and TurboTax for Mac (www.turbotax.com)	Online tax preparation site for state income taxes
Quicken Tax Freedom Project (QTFP) (www.quicken.com/freedom)	Free online tax preparation site for state income taxes
State-by-state tax sites—see Appendix B	
Federation of Tax Administrators (www.taxadmin.org/fta/rate/tax_stru.html)	State tax rates and structures
Tax Foundation (www.taxfoundation.org/pr-statelocal00.html)	A comparison of state taxes

Chapter 6

SITE	WHAT YOU'LL FIND
Quicken Tax Freedom Project (QTFP) (www.quicken.com/freedom)	Free online tax preparation site for state income taxes
IRS (www.irs.gov/prod/elec_srs/efile-ind.html)	Directory of *e-file* providers
FileYourTaxes.com (www.FileYourTaxes.com)	Online tax preparation site for state income taxes
Arkansas *Telefile* program (www.ar-tax.org)	Information on Arkansas' TeleFile program
Online sites for filing state returns— see Chapter 5	

Chapter 7

SITE	WHAT YOU'LL FIND
State-by-state sites for extension information—see Appendix B	

Chapter 8

SITE	WHAT YOU'LL FIND
IRS (www.irs.gov)	Information about EFTPS

Chapter 9

SITE	WHAT YOU'LL FIND
1-800FileTax (www.filetax.com)	Commercial tax filing services for business
Automatic Data Processing Inc. (ADP) (www.adp.com)	Payroll service provider
Biz.gov (www.tax.gov/1stop.htm)	Information on STAWRS program (one-step—federal and state— employment tax reporting)
C&S Technologies, Inc. (www.esmarttax.com)	Commercial tax filing services for business
Congressional Advisory Commission on Electronic Commerce (www.ecommercecommision.org)	Developments on taxation of e-commerce
Employers.gov (www.employers.gov/stawrs/index.htm)	Information on STAWRS program
ERISA Filing Acceptance System (EFAST) (www.efast.dol.gov)	List of approved vendors for EFAST (electronic filing of 5500 forms)

SITE	WHAT YOU'LL FIND
Federal Liaison Services (www.fls.com)	Payroll service provider
FileTaxes.Com (www.irsus.com/filetaxes.htm)	Commercial tax filing services for business
IRS (www.irs.gov/excise)	Excise taxes—general information
IRS (www.irs.gov)	Explanation of information return filing requirements (General Instructions for Forms 1099, 1098, 5498, and W-2G)
IRS (www.irs.gov)—click on "Small Business Corner"	Small Business Resource Guide on CD-ROM (information about it and online order form)
IRS (www.lrs.gov/bus_info/msu-info.html)	Information about Tip Rate Determination Agreement (TRDA) and Tip Reporting Alternative Commitment (TRAC) programs
IRS (www.irs.gov/elect_svs/abp.html)	Listing of IRS approved business *e-file* providers
IRS (www.irs.gov/elec_svs/fire-sys.html)	Information about the FIRE program
KPMG Peat Marwick (www.us.kpmg.com/salt/)	Information on taxing e-commerce
National Tax Online Inc. (www.nationtax.com)	Commercial tax filing services for business
Social Security Administration (SSA) (www.ssa.gov/employer/esohome.htm)	*E-filing* of Forms W-2 and W-3
Tax Cybrary (www.vertexinc.com/taxcybrary20/ taxcybrary_20.html)	Information an analysis on emerging issues on Internet taxation
TimeValue Software (www.taxpenalty.com)	Figure late payment penalties on employment taxes
U.S. Tax Center (www.center4debtmanagement.com/ Business Tax.shtml)	Commercial tax filing services for business

Chapter 10

SITE	WHAT YOU'LL FIND
1-800TaxFile (www.filetax.com)	Bookkeeping services and tax help
AccountantWeb (www.accountant.org)	Accounting resources

SITE	WHAT YOU'LL FIND
BAport Accounting (www.baport.com)	Online accounting
Deloitte & Touche Center for Multistate Taxation (www.uwm.edu/Dept/Business/MSTax/SALT	Information on state taxation for businesses
eLedger (www.eledger.com)	Online accounting
ePeachtree (www.epeachtree.com)	Online accounting
Gifts in Kind International (www.giftsinkind.org)	Clearinghouse for property donations
Intacct (www.intacct.com)	Online accounting
Intuit (www.quicken.com/small_business)	Information about accounting
IRS (www.irs.gov)	Per diem travel rates in Publication 1542
IRS (www.irs.gov/smallbiz/index.html)	IRS-sponsored small business web site
IRS (www.irs.gov/bus_info/mssp/index.html)	Audit guides
IRS (www.irs.gov/bus_info/pro/coord.html)	IRS coordinated issue papers
IRS Small Business Center (www.irs.gov)	Information about accounting
Microsoft bCentral (www.bcentral.com)	Information about accounting
National Association for Compensation Benefits and Total Rewards (www.worldatwork.org)	Surveys on skill-based pay, incentive pay, bonuses, and other benefits
National Association for Exchange of Industrial Resources (www.hvacmall.com/listing/naeir.htm)	Clearinghouse for property donations
NetLedger (www.netledger.com)	Online accounting
Policyworks (www.policyworks.gov)	Per diem travel rates
Salary.com (www.salary.com)	Pay scales for jobs in different metropolitan areas and states
CareerInfoNet (www.acinet.org)	Lists of salaries and benefits in different locations

Chapter 11

SITE	WHAT YOU'LL FIND
IRS (www.irs.gov) and (http://ftp.irs.gov)	Tax preparation material (forms, instructions, publications), tax research resources, answers to tax questions, news updates
IRS (www.irs.gov)—click on "Tax Info for You" and then "Spousal Tax Relief Eligibility Explorer"	Check eligibility for innocent spouse relief
IRS (www.irs.gov/hot/index.html)	Publication 553, Highlights of 2000 Tax Changes (view here for 2001 update)
IRS (www.irs.gov/bus_info/bullet.html)	Internal Revenue Bulletins
IRS (www.irs.gov/help/newmail/maillist.html)	Digital Dispatch (IRS online news publication)
IRS (www.irs.gov/help/newmail/user)	E-mail questions to the IRS
IRS (www.irs.gov/ind_info_advocate.html)	Information on the Taxpayer Advocate Service/Problem Resolution Office
IRS (www.irs.gov/prod/news/nandf.html)	Daily tax tip
IRS (www.irs.gov/tax_regs/index.html)	Plain English regulations
IRS (www.taxtalktoday.org)	Interactive series for professionals (continuing education credits available)
IRS' Freedom of Information Act office (www.irs.gov/prod/news/efoia/irs-online.html)	Private letter rulings, AODs, and other informal IRS pronouncements
IRS' Tax Trails (www.irs.gov/ind_info/tax_trails/index.html)	Interactive sessions on various tax topics
Re: Quest dot Net (www.re-Quest.net/financial/taxes/tax-forms/index.htm)	Tax forms
SecureTax.com (www.securetax.com)	Tax newsletters and other information
TaxAnalysts	Daily tax news
Tax Digest (www.taxdigest.com)	Electronic publication (mailed by e-mail)
TaxhelpOnline (www.taxhelponline.com)	Ask tax experts or attend online seminars

SITE	WHAT YOU'LL FIND
Tax Resources (www.taxresources.com)	Court decisions, Internal Revenue Code and regulations
Taxware International (www.taxware.com/news/newsinfo.htm)	News and information
U.S. Claims Court (www.taxresources.com)	U.S. Claims Court decisions
U.S. Supreme Court (www.supremecourtus.gov)	U.S. Supreme Court decisions
U.S. Tax Court (www.ustaxcourt.gov)	U.S. Tax Court decisions; court rules
UncleFed's Tax Board (www.unclefed.com)	Tax Court rules

Chapter 12

SITE	WHAT YOU'LL FIND
About.com (http://taxes.about.com/money/taxes/mbody.htm)	Tax web browser
American Institute of CPAs (AICPA) www.aicpa.org)	Search for accountant in your area
Arthur Andersen (www.arthurandersen.com)	Information for business on e-commerce/other tax information
Bloomberg Tax Guide (www.bloomberg.com/money/tax)	Online tax guide
Boardroom Inc. (www.bottomlinesecrets.com)	Articles about tax developments and strategies
BWideas.com (www.bwideas.com)	Monthly ideas for small business
CCH Inc. (http://Onlinestore.cch.com)	Tax news, information, and related products
CPAdirectory (www.cpadirectory.com)	Search for accountant by name, city, state, zip code
DejaNews (www.deja.com)	Search old messages at newsgroups
Deloitte & Touche LLP (www.dtonline.com)	Developments affecting federal, state, and local taxes
Dennis Schmidt's State and Local Taxes (www.taxsites.com/state.html)	Links to state tax information
El.com (Essential Links to Taxes) (www.el.com/dir/cat_taxes.asp?tree=126)	Tax web browser

SITE	WHAT YOU'LL FIND
Ernst & Young (www.ey.com)	Library of articles on various topics
Excite (www.excite.com/apple/guide/Money/Taxes/)	Tax web browser
FindLaw (www.findlaw.com)	U.S. Supreme Court decisions, other cases, and regulations
Firstgov (www.firstgov.gov)	Links to state and local governments
iFigure (www.ifigure.com/money/taxes/taxes.htm)	Tax web browser
Internet Directory of Tax Professionals (www.tax-directory.com)	Listing of tax professionals
Jurisline.com (www.jurisline.com)	Internal Revenue Code and regulations
KPMG Peat Marwick (www.us.kpmg.com/services/tax/index.html)	Links to other tax sites
Law.freeadvice.com (www.law.freeadvice.com/tax_law)	Tax advice
Lawyers.com (from Martindale-Hubbell) (www.lawyers.com)	Search for attorney
Legal Information Institute at Cornell Law School (www.4law.cornell.edu/uscode/23) (www.law.cornell.edu/opinions.html)	Internal Revenue Code Decisions from federal and state courts
MyCounsel.com (www.mycounsel.com)	Legal referral site
MyLawyer.com (www.mylawyer.com)	Legal information (including tax Information)
National Association of Tax Professionals (www.taxprofessionals.com)	Search for public accountant
Newsgroup: Misc.taxes (http://misc.taxes.moderated.com)	Moderated tax discussion groups
Nolo.com (www.nolo.com)	View tax topics
Pricewaterhouse Coopers Lybrand (www.taxnews.com)	Tax news
Research Institute of America (RIA) (www.ria.com)	Tax news and information
SmartMoney.com Tax Guide (www.smartmoney.com/tax)	Online tax guide
Tax Harbor Tax Guide (www.taxharbor.com)	Online tax guide

SITE	WHAT YOU'LL FIND
Tax Logic (www.taxlogic.com)	Submit questions online to tax professionals
TaxMama (www.taxmamma.com/IRSnews)	Online newsletter
TaxNet USA, Inc. (www.taxnetusa.com)	Property tax information
Tax Resources (www.taxresources.com)	Tax web browser
TaxTopic.com (www.taxtopic.com)	Online research portal for federal and state taxes
TaxUp (www.taxup.com)	State tax information by location; global tax information
TaxWeb (www.taxweb.com)	Tax web browser; links to tax information
ThatHomeSite (www.thathomesite.com/forums/taxes)	Chat room devoted to the topic of taxes
Touro Law School (www.tourolaw.edu/AboutTLC/courts)	Information on and decisions from federal courts
TRAC (data-gathering organization associated with Syracuse University) (http://trac.syr.edu/tracirs)	Check audit risk based on income, location, and other factors
Uchats.com (www.uchats.com)	Chat room search engine
University of Chicago Law Lists (www.lib.uchicago.edu/cgi-bin/law-lists)—click on "tax" to find groups	Tax discussion groups
USLaw.com (www.uslaw.com)	Online chats with attorneys (for a fee)
U.S. Tax Court On-Line (www.fourmilab.ch/ustax/ustax.html)	Internal Revenue Code

Chapter 13

SITE	WHAT YOU'LL FIND
Banksite.com (www.banksite.com/calc/estate)	Federal estate tax calculator
Bloomberg (www.bloomberg.com)	Federal estate tax calculator
Charitygift (www.charitygift.com)	Database of charitable organizations
Charles Schwab (www.schwab.com)—go to Planning	Retirement planning information

SITE	WHAT YOU'LL FIND
CNNfn (http://cnnfn.cnn.com/markets/ personalfinance/	Advice on investing and taxes; retirement planning
Computers for Schools Association (www.detwiler.org)	Organizations accepting donations of used computers
Computers for Youth (www.cfy.org)	Organizations accepting donations of used computers
Donate a Phone (www.donateaphone.com)	Organizations accepting donations of used cell phones
DonateTo.com (www.DonateTo.com)	Database of charitable organizations
Ed Slott's IRA Help (www.irahelp.com)	Rules on minimum required distributions from qualified plans and IRAs
Entrepreneur Magazine (www.entreprenuer.com)	General tax planning information for small business
Estate Web! (www.estateweb.com/common/calc. htm)	Federal estate tax calculator
Fairmark (www.fairmark.com)	Free tax guide for investors
Fidelity (www.fidelity.com) (www100.fidelity.com) (http://web400.fidelity.com/legacy/ index.htm)	College savings calculator Information on 529 plans for college savings Federal estate tax calculator
GainsKeeper (www.gainskeeper.com)	Online program for alerting investor when to sell/online tracking of investments (cost: $49 to $299/year)
GE Center for Financial Learning (www.financiallearning.com)	Tax implications of investing
General Accounting Office (www.gao.gov/new.items/ggoo180. pdf)	Information on AMT
Guidestar (www.guidestar.com)	Database of charitable organizations
H&R Block (www.hrblock.com/taxes/index.html)	General tax planning information for individuals
Inc.com (www.inc.com)	General tax planning information for small business
InvestingInBonds.com (www.investinginbonds.com)	Comparable of taxable to tax-free bonds

SITE	WHAT YOU'LL FIND
IRS (www.irs.gov) (www.irs.gov/prod/bus_info/eo/eosearch. html)	**Publication 561 for determining the value of donated property Information on AMT in Publication 17 Online database of tax exempt organizations**
Kelley Blue Book (www.kbb.com)	**Determine the value of used car donations**
Money (www.money.com)	**Articles from *Money* magazine on investments (including tax issues)**
Morningstar (www.morningstar.com)	**Information on mutual funds' tax efficiency**
Motley Fool (www.fool.com or AOL keyword: fool)	**General investment information, including rules on capital gains and losses**
MSN Money Central (www.msn.com/investments)	**General investment information, including rules on capital gains and losses**
MSN Money Central Taxes (http://moneycentral.msn.com/tax/home.asp)	**General tax planning information for individuals**
MyStockOptions.com (www.mystockoptions.com)	**Explanation of the tax rules on stock options and valuation methods**
NASD Investor Services Calculators (http://investor.nasd.com/gamec/default.html)	**College savings calculator**
Natalie B. Choate, Esq. (www.ataxplan.com/articles_fr/dist_ rules.htm)	**Rules on minimum required distributions from qualified plans and IRAs**
National Cristina Foundation (www.cristina.org)	**Organizations accepting donations of used computers**
New York College Savings Program (www.nysaves.org)	**Information on NY's 529 plan for college savings**
Office.com (www.office.com)	**General tax planning information for small business**
Pension Rights Center (www.pensionrights.org)	**Help in deciding on retirement plan payout options**
PEP National Directory of Computer Recycling Programs (www.microweb.com/pepsite)	**Organizations accepting donations of used computers**
PersonalFund.com (www.personalfund.com/index.html)	**Information on mutual funds' tax efficiency**
Quicken.com (www.quicken.com)—go to Business News and Money News (www.quicken.com/investments)	**Retirement planning information** **Basic information about capital gains and losses—free**

SITE	WHAT YOU'LL FIND
Robert Keebler (www.rothira.com)	Rules on minimum required distributions from qualified plans and IRAs
SEC Mutual Fund Calculator (www.sec.gov/mfcc/mfcc-int.htm)	Information on mutual funds' tax efficiency
Seymour Goldberg, Esq, CPA (www.goldbergira.com)	Rules on minimum required distributions from qualified plans and IRAs
Smarleaf Advisor (www.smartleaf.com)	Free calculator for determining when to take a loss (online advisory service at $20/month)
SmartMoney (www.smartmoney.com/tax/capital/index.cfm?story=amt)	AMT estimator
(www.smartmoney.com/tax/capital/index.cfm?story=estate)	Estate tax calculator
(www.smartmoney.com/tax/capital/index.cfm?story=options)	Stock options calculator
(www.smartmoney.com)	Tax implications about investing
Social Security Administration (SSA) (www.ssa.gov/retire)	Online calculator for projecting Social Security benefits
TaxPlanet.com (www.taxplanet.com)	General tax planning information for individuals
TIAA-CREF (www.tiaa-cref.org)	529 plans for college savings
TradersAccounting.com (www.tradersaccounting.com)	MS Excel spreadsheet that can be used as an attachment on Schedule D
T.Rowe Price (www3.troweprice.com/cftools/CPC/index.cfm)	College savings calculator
(www.troweprice.com/tools/toolsInsight/Home.html)	Roth IRA conversion calculator
U.S. Bureau of Labor Statistics (www.bls.gov)	Online inflation calculator
U.S. Bureau of Public Debt (www.savingsbonds.gov/sav/savcalc.htm)	Find redemption values for savings bonds
U.S. Bureau of Public Debt (www.savingsbonds.gov/sav/savwizar.htm)	Download wizard for keeping track of savings bond holdings
USA Today (www.usatoday.com/money/calculat/mcfront.htm)	College savings calculator
UsedComputer.com (www.usedcomputer.com)	Determine the value of computer donations

SITE	WHAT YOU'LL FIND
Vanguard (www.vanguard.com/cgi-bin/RothConv)	Roth IRA conversion calculator
Women's Wire (www.womenswire.com/money)	Advice on investing, geared toward single women
Yahoo Tax Center (http://taxes/yahoo.com/)	General tax planning information for individuals

Directory of State Revenue Departments

STATE	WEB SITE	TELEPHONE NUMBER
Alabama	www.ador.state.al.us	334-242-1170
Alaska	www.revenue.state.ak.us/	907-269-6620
Arizona	www.revenue.state.az.us/	602-542-4260
Arkansas	www.state.ar.us/dfa	501-682-7250
California	www.ftb.ca.gov	800-338-0505
Colorado	www.revenue.state.co.us	303-232-2414
Connecticut	www.drs.state.ct.us	800-382-9463 860-297-5962
Delaware	www.state.de.us/revenue	302-577-8200
District of Columbia	www.dccfo.com	202-442-4829
Florida	www.state.fl.us/	850-488-6800
Georgia	www2.state.ga.us/departments/DOR	404-656-4293
Hawaii	www.state.hi.us/tax/tax.html	800-222-7572
Idaho	www.state.id.us.tax	800-972-7660
Illinois	www.revenue.state.il.us	800-356-6302 217-785-3400

STATE	WEB SITE	TELEPHONE NUMBER
Indiana	www.in.gov/dor/	317-615-2581
Iowa	www.state.ia.us/government/drf/	800-532-1531 515-281-7239
Kansas	www.ink.org/public/kdor	785-296-4937
Kentucky	www.state.ky.us/	502-564-3658
Louisiana	www.rev.state.la.us	225-925-7532
Maine	http://janus.state.me.us/revenue	207-626-8475
Maryland	www.marylandtaxes.com	410-260-7951
Massachusetts	www. state.ma.us/tax.htm	800-392-6089 617-887-6367
Michigan	www.treas.state.mi.us	800-367-6263
Minnesota	www.taxes.state.mn.us	800-657-3676 612-296-4444
Mississippi	www.mstc.state.ms.us	601-923-7800
Missouri	www.dor.state.mo.us	800-877-6881
Montana	www.state.mt.us/revenue/	406-444-6900
Nebraska	www.nol.org/home/NDR	402-471-5729
Nevada	www.state.nv.us	775-687-4892
New Hampshire	www.state.nh.us	603-271-2192
New Jersey	www.state.nj.us/treasury/taxation	800-323-4400
New Mexico	www.state.nm.us/tax	505-827-2206
New York	www.tax.state.ny.us	800-462-8100
North Carolina	www.dor.state.nc.us	919-715-0397
North Dakota	www.state.nd.us/taxdpt	800-638-2901 701-328-3450
Ohio	www.state.oh.us/tax	614-846-6712
Oklahoma	www.oktax.state.ok.us/	405-521-3108
Oregon	www.dor.state.or.us	403-378-4988
Pennsylvania	www.revenue.state.pa.us	888-PATAXES
Rhode Island	www.dor.state.ri.us	401-222-1111
South Carolina	www.dor.state.sc.us	800-768-3676
South Dakota	www.state.sd.us/treasurer	605-773-3378
Texas	www.window.state.tx.us	1-888-4FILING
Tennessee	www.state.tn.us/revenue	800-342-1003 615-253-0600

STATE	WEB SITE	TELEPHONE NUMBER
Utah	www.tax.ex.state.ut.us	801-297-2200
Vermont	www.state.vt.us/tax	802-828-2865
Virginia	www.state.va.us/tax/tax.html	804-367-8055
West Virginia	www.state.wv.us/taxrev/	304-344-2068
Wisconsin	www.dor.state.wi.us	608-266-1961
Wyoming	http://revenue.state.wy.us	307-777-7961

Index